Waste and Recycling

ISSUES
(formerly Issues for the Nineties)

Volume 14

Editor

Craig Donnellan

Independence
Educational Publishers
Cambridge

First published by Independence
PO Box 295
Cambridge CB1 3XP
England

British Library Cataloguing in Publication Data
Waste and Recycling – (Issues Series)
I. Donnellan, Craig II. Series
363.7'28

ISBN 1 86168 128 3

Printed in Great Britain
The Burlington Press
Cambridge

Typeset by
Claire Boyd

Cover
The illustration on the front cover is by
Pumpkin House.

CONTENTS

Chapter One: The Problems of Waste

Chapter Two: Reducing Waste

Introduction

Waste and Recycling is the fourteenth volume in the **Issues** series. The aim of this series is to offer up-to-date information about important issues in our world.

Waste and Recycling looks at the problems caused by waste and ways of reducing waste.

The information comes from a wide variety of sources and includes:
Government reports and statistics
Newspaper reports and features
Magazine articles and surveys
Literature from lobby groups
and charitable organisations.

It is hoped that, as you read about the many aspects of the issues explored in this book, you will critically evaluate the information presented. It is important that you decide whether you are being presented with facts or opinions. Does the writer give a biased or an unbiased report? If an opinion is being expressed, do you agree with the writer?

Waste and Recycling offers a useful starting-point for those who need convenient access to information about the many issues involved. However, it is only a starting-point. At the back of the book is a list of organisations which you may want to contact for further information.

*****

Rubbish

Information from the Young People's Trust for the Environment

We produce more rubbish today than ever before, on average each household in Britain produces about a tonne of waste every year. Much of this waste contains potentially useful materials such as paper and board, glass, metals and textiles which could be recycled, reducing the amount of rubbish, creating less pollution and saving energy.

Rubbish

The amount of rubbish we produce has been escalating over the last 40 years. There has been a gradual change in shopping habits and people's attitudes to throwing things away. The personal service provided by shopkeepers has been replaced by self-service in supermarkets where the goods are often highly packaged; often loose items are packed together and priced to speed up payment at the check-outs. Some goods are elaborately wrapped to make them look more attractive, put into plastic bags and then loaded into plastic carrier bags at the check-out. A Women's Environmental Network group bought a trolley-load of 102 basic items – the shopping for a family for two weeks. They found that there was a total of 543 pieces of packaging with some items wrapped in up to five layers!

On average a family of four throws away about two sacks of rubbish a week, most of which could be recycled. The figures below show the main constituents of household waste:

- Paper and card 30%
- Kitchen waste 30%
- Glass 10%
- Metal 10%
- Plastic 8%

The amounts are quite staggering. Each person in a year generates 10 times their own weight in household rubbish, throwing away 90 drink cans, 107 bottles and jars, two trees' worth of paper, 70 food cans and 45kg of plastic.

Landfill

Ninety per cent of domestic waste in the UK goes directly to landfill or dumping sites to be levelled and covered with earth. This costs about £1 million a day. Once the rubbish has been covered the organic matter starts to rot down producing methane, an inflammable gas, which makes its way to the surface. In some tips the methane is piped off and used as fuel for heating. Landfill waste remains a potential environmental hazard. Weed-killers in the rubbish, chemicals from car batteries and other dangerous liquids can be washed through the soil, contaminating drinking water. In landfill sites where toxic industrial wastes have been dumped indiscriminately, the land can become poisoned and unsafe for farming or building. Today, waste disposal is regulated by a number of European Community directives which help to ensure that the disposal of waste is controlled and safe.

Incineration

Ten per cent of all domestic waste is burned in waste incinerators but this method of disposal can be hazardous. If the temperature in the incinerator is allowed to fall below 900°C, some plastics, pesticides and wood preservatives can produce dioxins which are extremely poisonous.

Action

You could make a survey of what is thrown away at home using bar graphs to keep records. This will give some idea of the enormous amount of resources which are thrown away each week.

Packaging

Packaging materials make up about 10% of household waste. Traditional materials like waxed card and paper have been replaced by foamed plastics, aluminium and polythene. The result is a high volume of lightweight rubbish which swamps litter bins, blows about in the wind and is, in the main, non biodegradable.

Packaging has three main purposes: protection, preservation, and to make the product look more attractive to potential buyers. Many packaging materials are combined together in such a way that they are impossible to separate and therefore cannot be recycled.

Action

If there is no choice, buy products which are contained in the least amount of packaging. Buying in bulk helps since items packaged in small quantities produce more waste than those packaged in large quantities. Packaging made of paper or cardboard is preferable to plastic and glass bottles are better than plastic ones, especially if they are returnable.

The problem of plastic

More than 2 million tonnes of plastics are used in the UK each year, making up a further 10% of household rubbish. Nearly all the plastics in use are made from oil and resist any form of biological decomposition. These are non-biodegradable plastics and cause problems in waste incineration since many of them give off poisonous gases when burned. Biodegradable plastics which are made from sugar and other carbohydrates rot away within months of being buried. However, the cost of biodegradable plastics is far greater than that of ordinary plastics since their production is carried out on a small scale. If biodegradable plastics were widely used in preference to other plastics manufacturing costs would drop dramatically.

• The above information is an extract from the Young People's Trust for the Environment web site which can be found at www.yptenc.org.uk

Household rubbish problem is piling up

*By Charles Clover,
Environment Editor*

A rubbish mountain of consumer waste caused by obsolete computers, ready-cooked meals in trays and newspaper supplements was a problem, the Government admitted yesterday.

It gave itself another five years to meet the target set by the Tories a decade ago of recycling a quarter of every dustbin's rubbish by the year 2000.

A three-per-cent-a-year rise in household waste could lead to the near doubling of the annual waste mountain of 27 million tons in 20 years.

Michael Meacher, the environment minister, said that, if waste collection continued at the current rate, Britain would hit 'a crisis' and he forecast that as many as 130 new incinerators could be needed.

'We must all take more responsibility for cutting the waste we generate,' he said. 'This means thinking not only about how we manage waste but also how we can use it as a resource.'

He was launching a draft waste strategy which sets targets of recovering 45 per cent of municipal waste by 2010 – for incineration with heat recovery, recycling and composting. It also sets the target of recycling or composting 30 per cent of household waste by 2010.

Currently Britain recycles eight per cent of its municipal waste and is expected to miss the 25 per cent target by more than half.

'The situation facing waste management in Britain is extremely serious and will require a change in behaviour and practice'

More waste, between 70 and 100 million tons a year, comes from industry and commerce. The Government proposes to cut the amount landfilled to 85 per cent of 1998 levels by 2005.

'The situation facing waste management in Britain is extremely serious and will require a change in behaviour and practice,' said a report by the Market Development Group Mr Meacher published along with the waste strategy.

The group, which is trying to build markets for recycled products, said that only 3.3 million tons of packaging waste were recovered last year.

One problem preventing more recycling was the British custom of importing millions of bottles of green glass full of wine but using only clear glass for milk bottles.

Solutions proposed include a reduction in the amount of imported green glass and the use of recycled green glass for milk bottles.

What is waste?

Information from the Industry Council for Packaging and the Environment (INCPEN)

Waste is anything that is no longer useful and needs to be got rid of.

It is defined by the type of place in which it is produced – like household, industrial or clinical – and how dangerous it is.

Waste is always with us

It is a well-known law of physics that matter cannot be created or destroyed. We can change its physical (solid, liquid or gas) or chemical form, but we cannot make it disappear.

If you throw something away it does not disappear:

- It may be burned but it is still there as gases, ash and heat.
- It may be buried (landfilled) so that it is decomposed by bacteria, but that still leaves the rotted materials and produces gases.
- It may stay where it is.

But it will not disappear.

Everything we use is originally made from resources from the earth and oceans and the gases of the atmosphere. Eventually everything returns either to the earth, to the oceans or to the atmosphere.

There are many ways of handling waste, including reusing and recycling it, but finally all materials end up as waste and are disposed of either to land, water or air.

One person's waste is another person's raw material

It is very difficult to get information about exactly how much waste there is. This is partly because it is human nature to want to ignore something that is no longer useful, so very little waste is actually measured. But it is also because what is waste in one place can be a resource somewhere else.

For example, from the brewer's point of view the spent yeast from the brewing of beer is waste.

In Burton-on-Trent, there are a number of breweries that produce this yeast. The Marmite factory in Burton-on-Trent takes it and converts it into Marmite yeast extract. If you look at the ingredients list on a jar of Marmite, you will see the main ingredient is 'yeast extract'. Since 1902 the breweries' waste has been used as the raw material for Marmite.

What waste is not

Waste is not litter – even though many people confuse the two. We get waste from all sorts of activities. If it is managed properly we need never have litter. Litter is simply badly managed – or unmanaged – waste. It is waste that is left lying around. It therefore attracts attention and is far more visible than managed waste.

An American archaeologist who calls himself a 'garbologist' and digs up landfilled waste, explains one of the things that happens when litter is confused with waste:

'What we think is in landfills and what happens to it over time is based more on fantasies than on facts. In fact, our visions of solid waste seem to be based on what we see every day as litter. For example, people who have never seen the inside of a landfill, but have seen much advertising and litter, reckon that packaging from fast foods makes up 20%-30% of waste (the reality is less than 1%).'

Recycling waste will not solve the litter problem because the people who care enough about the environment to take part in collecting materials for recycling are likely to be careful and thoughtful about how they dispose of all waste.

People who drop litter are the opposite; they do not care enough even to make sure waste is properly discarded. They are very unlikely to take the extra effort needed to collect for recycling.

• The above is an extract from the web site of the Industry Council for Packaging and the Environment (INCPEN) which can be found at www.incpen.org.uk

What do we mean by waste?

Information from Biffa

As an outcome of every production process, waste is an inescapable consequence of a consumer society. As such waste is a 'product' like any other.

An average British family:

- generates 0.59 tonnes per annum from its dustbin;
- has a further 3.6 tonnes produced on its behalf by industry and commerce;
- a further 15 tonnes by agriculture, mining, quarrying and construction

Waste is also a paradoxical product. It demands contrary thinking. Companies need to minimise its production and pay 'buyers' to take it away. However, waste is not a homogeneous commodity. Waste streams are complex, presenting several different disposal challenges. Companies need to buy a package of services to handle all aspects in an efficient and responsible fashion. Yet because waste is unwanted, otherwise well-run firms tend to ignore a fundamental management principle that governs all other areas of their businesses.

All areas of potential cost or profit should be the subject of a clear business strategy.

Our MORI survey reveals that despite the importance of waste as a future cost driver for business, and despite the personal liability of directors for their waste under the Environment Protection Act (EPA), it is very rare that a company's waste policy is directly the province of a board director.

Waste is not, in itself, a bad thing; rather it is poor waste management that is wasteful and sometimes dangerous. Professionally handled waste presents no threat to people or their environment.

A healthy society is not one which produces no waste, but one which recognises its duty to manage, not ignore, its waste.

We all, society and industry together, have a responsibility to manage waste with an eye to the future, to avoid the threats of pollution, disease and environmental blight.

What is waste?

Waste can be classified in three ways:

- According to where it comes from – 'arisings'
- According to its pollution potential – 'environmental impact'
- According to its state – 'liquid or solid or gaseous'

'Arisings'

Waste may be classified according to its source. The Department of the Environment estimates that dry waste arisings in the UK total around 400 million tonnes per year.

'Environmental impact'

Waste may be classified according to its environmental impact.

- Inert: 39% (159m tonnes) of total waste arisings are inert, e.g. glass, plastic, metals, rubble
- Hazardous (special): 1% (2.5m tonnes) of total waste arisings are hazardous, e.g. laboratory waste, spent chemicals
- Putrescible: 60% (239m tonnes) of total waste arisings are putrescible, e.g. unconsumed food, agricultural waste, sewage

'Liquid, solid or gaseous'

Waste may be classified according to its state: liquid, solid or gaseous

No one knows the total levels of liquid waste arisings in the UK – although some three and a half billion tonnes of waste water are treated in sewage works each year. The bulk of industrial effluents is currently discharged to water courses, the sea, or even by some operators into landfill. Only the volume to landfill is known with confidence – three million tonnes.

Increasing volumes are undergoing sophisticated treatments. Handling and the transportation of liquid waste presents a different sort of challenge to solid waste.

The total volume of gaseous emissions in the UK is also difficult to quantify. However, total annual CO_2 emissions from industry are 160 million tonnes – or one and a half times the amount of waste sent each year to landfill.

- Reproduced by kind permission of HTI Leadership & Management. HTI is an educational charity which aims to enchance leadership and management within schools. This material was sourced from HTI's environmental educational site, Education for Sustainability, which can be found at www.e4s.org.uk

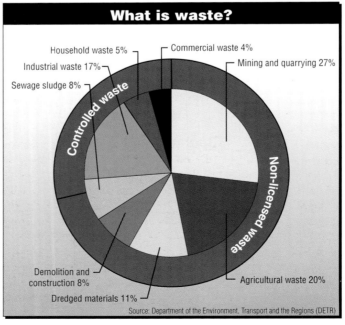

What is waste?

Household waste 5%
Commercial waste 4%
Industrial waste 17%
Mining and quarrying 27%
Sewage sludge 8%
Controlled waste
Non-licensed waste
Demolition and construction 8%
Agricultural waste 20%
Dredged materials 11%

Source: Department of the Environment, Transport and the Regions (DETR)

Facts on waste

Are you doing your bit?

- The volume of waste produced in the UK in one hour would fill the Albert Hall.
  (Source: LGB Publications)

- In one day there would be enough waste to fill Trafalgar Square up to the top of Nelson's Column.
  (Source: LGB Publications)

- In one year there would be enough waste to fill dustbins stretching from the Earth to the moon.
  (Source: LGB Publications)

Metals (e.g. food and drink cans)

- Every year in the UK we use 13 billion steel cans which, placed end to end, would stretch to the moon – three times!
  (Source: Steel Can Recycling Information Bureau)

- Every year 13 billion steel cans are produced and up to a quarter of every new steel can is made from recycled steel. This is the equivalent of over 3 billion cans made from recycled material.
  (Source: Steel Can Recycling Information Bureau)

- Producing steel from recycled materials saves 75 per cent of the energy needed to make steel from virgin materials.
  (Source: Steel Can Recycling Information Bureau)

- Recycling aluminium can bring energy savings of up to 95%, reduces import costs, and produces 95% less greenhouse gas emissions than when it is produced from raw materials.
  (Source: alupro)

- About 20,000 tonnes of aluminium foil packaging (worth £8 million) is wasted every year. Only 3,000 tonnes is recycled (worth £1.2 million).
  (Source: alupro)

- If all the aluminium cans sold in the UK were recycled, there would be 12 million fewer full dustbins each year.
  (Source: Alucan website)

Paper (e.g. newspapers and magazines)

- Each tonne of paper recycled saves 15 average-sized trees, as well as their surrounding habitat and wildlife.
  (Source: World Wildlife Fund)

- Reclaimed waste paper represents around 63% of the fibre used to produce paper and board in the UK.
  (Source: The Paper & Pulp Information Centre)

Glass (e.g. glass bottles and jars)

- Glass packaging makes up about 9% by weight of the average household dustbin but accounts for over 70% by weight of packaging recycled from the total household waste stream.
  (Source: British Glass)

- Up to 90% of new glass can be made from reclaimed scrap glass, which saves energy and raw materials.
  (Source: British Glass)

- In the UK, we use over 6 billion glass containers each year, equating to over 2 million tonnes. In 1998 we recycled 22% of these containers – the European average is 50%, with some countries recycling over 80%. (Source: British Glass)

- There are 22,000 bottle bank sites in the UK.
  (Source: British Glass)

Plastic (e.g. carrier bags and plastic bottles and pots)

- It is estimated that if 30% of the current consumption of thermo-plastics in the UK could be recycled to replace virgin raw materials, substantial energy savings would be achieved and carbon dioxide emissions would be reduced by about 3 million tonnes/year. (Source: ETSU)

- Of the 2.4 million tonnes of plastic waste, an estimated 1,400,000 tonnes is household plastic waste, 200,000 tonnes is 'process scrap', and 800,000 tonnes is commercial waste. 61% of the total plastic waste from Western Europe is packaging, which typically has a 'life' of less than 12 months.

(Source: AEA Technology)

Packing generally

- Packaging is typically 25-35% by weight of dustbin waste, but developments in material strength and manufacturing technologies have allowed less material to contain the same volume of goods. Compared to 50 years ago:
– food cans are 50% lighter;

– yoghurt pots are 60% lighter;
– glass milk bottles are 50% lighter;
– plastic carrier bags are half as thick;
Reducing the weight of packaging saves on transport costs and emissions as well as reducing consumption of raw materials.

(Source: INCPEN)

Other household waste (e.g. kitchen food scraps, books and unwanted toys)

- About a third of household waste is kitchen and garden waste – help reduce it by adding vegetable

peelings and fruit skins to your compost heap.

(Source: INCPEN)

- Another third of the dustbin is paper – ask your dentist or doctor if they would like old magazines for their waiting room and support paper recycling schemes.

(Source: INCPEN)

- Your waste can have a value to someone else – take old clothes, books, toys and bric-a-brac to charity shops or car boot sales.

(Source: INCPEN)

© Crown Copyright

Britain to be 'swamped' by rubbish

By Michael McCarthy, Environment Correspondent

Britain faces a 'mammoth task' dealing with its yearly 25 million tonnes of household waste, a figure expected to double over 20 years, Michael Meacher, the Environment Minister, said yesterday.

A tough new European law means that soon most of the refuse will have to be diverted away from rubbish dumps. Launching the Government's draft waste strategy, Mr Meacher said radical targets for waste recycling and recovery would have to be set.

In the next six years, local councils will have to triple the amount of household waste they recycle, from 8 per cent to 25 per cent of the total, and between 40 and 130 big waste incinerators might have to be built. Friends of the Earth vowed to fight an incinerator building programme. 'People don't want these monsters,' said Mike Childs, its waste campaigner. 'Intensive recycling is the way forward.'

Britain's domestic refuse heap is increasing by 3 per cent a year largely because of our throwaway society, which jettisons millions of takeaway food cartons annually, as well as rapidly obsolescent electronic equipment, and an

enormous pile of newspaper supplements.

The EU landfill directive requires the amount of UK household waste ending up in rubbish tips to be cut from the present 85 per cent to no more than 35 per cent by 2020. The Government calculates that, by then, 35 million tonnes of rubbish might have to be accommodated elsewhere than on rubbish tips each year.

By 2005, the Government also wants to get 40 per cent of household waste 'recovered' – using recycling, composting and incineration to

The Government calculates that, by 2020, 35 million tonnes of rubbish might have to be accommodated elsewhere than on rubbish tips each year

recover energy or heat. At the moment only 14 per cent of energy is recovered, but that figure should rise to 66 per cent by 2015.

Landfill for the country's industrial and commercial waste – between 70 and 100 million tonnes a year – will have to be cut to 85 per cent of the 1998 figure by 2005, the Government says. Recycling will be boosted by government help for the recycled materials markets. A study group has been set up to work on recycling schemes and Mr Meacher indicated that the Government might intervene to guarantee prices.

The need for the strategy was 'stark', Mr Meacher said yesterday. 'We are rapidly running out of landfill spaces. We need a major sustained change in public attitudes to the creation of waste.' In the Netherlands 45 per cent of household waste is recycled; in Switzerland the figure is 42 per cent and, in the United States, 31 per cent.

- The Government has abandoned a 'variable charging' plan – higher bills for more waste removed – which has been criticised as a waste tax.

© The Independent July, 1999

The management of wastes

Information from the Environment Agency

A major pressure on the environment arises from the wastes produced as a by-product of industrial and domestic activities. The Environment Agency is responsible for regulating the treatment, storage and disposal of controlled wastes, which consist of industrial, household, and commercial waste but exclude mine and quarry wastes, wastes from premises used for agriculture, sewage sludge (except that disposed to landfill), radioactive waste and explosives. Household, commercial and industrial wastes are specifically defined under the Environmental Protection Act (Controlled Waste) Regulations (SI 1992, No 588). Special waste is any controlled waste consisting of, or contaminated with, substances which make it 'dangerous to life' as defined in the Control of Pollution (Special Waste) Regulation 1980 (SI 1980, No 1709).

Waste statistics for England and Wales are not readily available. The Department of Environment publication *Digest of Environmental Protection Statistics No 17* (1995) indicates that in 1990 approximately 435 million tonnes of waste were produced in the UK. About 245 million tonnes of this was controlled waste. The Agency will be charged with carrying out a national waste survey under the Environment Act

1995, in order to develop further the DOE's initial waste management strategy.

The UK uses a waste management hierarchy of waste reduction, reuse, recovery (recycling, composting or converting into energy) or, if these options are not viable, disposal. It is obviously most cost effective to prevent arisings of waste in the first place. This is achieved by industry carrying out life-cycle analyses of a particular product to examine opportunities for waste minimisation and involves examining an activity to seek ways of minimising wastes or reusing by-products. Consumer products can also be recycled after use: for example glass bottles, steel cans, aluminium cans and paper and board. Even when discarded, some materials can be recovered for recycling, such as scrap metals. There is an increasing trend towards recovering energy from waste, either by burning it or by using the methane-rich gas generated as organic wastes decompose in landfills. It is estimated that at present some 21% of controlled waste in the UK is recycled or reused, and the Government has set targets of 25% by the year 2000.

By far the greatest proportion (70%) of controlled waste (excluding sewage sludge and dredged spoils) in the UK is currently sent to landfill.

In 1993/94 in England and Wales a total of 2,784 landfill sites were licensed, landfill being regarded as the only option for some inert wastes and for wastes that are difficult to burn or recycle. But regardless of how well they are located and engineered, landfills have the potential to release chemicals into surface and underground water, and soil, and to generate significant quantities of methane, which is a 'greenhouse gas'. Some 45% of the total methane emissions in the UK are currently estimated as arising from landfills. During the operation of landfill sites, noise, odour, unsightliness and vehicle movements may cause a local nuisance. After landfilling, the land may retain contaminants and be unsuitable for some uses.

Control of waste management activities is regulated via Part 2 of the Environmental Protection Act 1990. The Agency carries forward the responsibilities of some 83 separate Waste Regulation Authorities to license the operation of waste disposal, recovery and treatment operations. The Agency will also have a formal role in providing advice on the Government's waste strategy, which is required for the purposes of Article 7 of the EC Waste Framework Directive, and will be responsible for implementing a scheme of 'producer

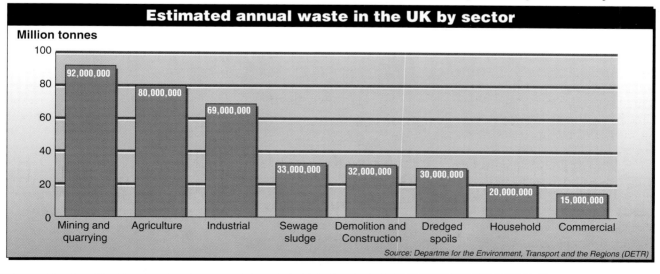

Estimated annual waste in the UK by sector

Million tonnes

- Mining and quarrying: 92,000,000
- Agriculture: 80,000,000
- Industrial: 69,000,000
- Sewage sludge: 33,000,000
- Demolition and Construction: 32,000,000
- Dredged spoils: 30,000,000
- Household: 20,000,000
- Commercial: 15,000,000

Source: Departme for the Environment, Transport and the Regions (DETR)

responsibility' with regard to waste reduction by industry under the Environment Act 1995.

The safe disposal of human biological waste is essential both for human health and environmental reasons. England and Wales are relatively well sewered, with over 96% of the population connected to a waste water collection system in 1995. Some 80% of the population has its waste water treated to a secondary or tertiary level before it is returned to the environment. At present, the sludge arising from the treatment of this waste water is disposed of by four principal routes: by application to farmland; by disposal to landfills; by dumping at sea; and by incineration. Some 196,000 tonnes of sewage sludge are currently disposed of at sea each year, but this practice will cease by the end of 1998.

Approximately 473,000 tonnes of sewage sludge is added to agricultural land each year. This practice is controlled by the Agency through regulations (SI 1989/1263) which implement the EC Directive on Sewage Sludge in Agriculture (86/278/EEC). The regulations require that no one, including the farmer or the supplier of the sludge, may permit the use of sewage sludge on agricultural land unless certain requirements are fulfilled. This is to safeguard, particularly, against the addition of excessive levels of metals to the soil.

The Agency is looking at the management of different waste streams. For example a report on the impact of tyres in the environment considers the options for dealing with worn tyres in the context of a wider environmental strategy.

© *Environment Agency*

The present day

Information from Waste Watch

Today in the UK, it is estimated that each household will throw away over a tonne of waste every year, totalling around 26 million tonnes. For every tonne of waste we produce in our homes, it is estimated that 5 tonnes of waste has already been created at the manufacturing stage, and 20 tonnes at the point where the raw material was extracted.

On average every person in the UK throws away their own body weight in rubbish every three months.

Potentially 50% by weight of dustbin contents is recyclable. Another 20% is made up of compostable organic material. On average only 5% of dustbin contents is recycled despite the fact that surveys show that over 90% of people think that recycling is important. This means that we could recycle ten times as much as we do now. By contrast 83% of household waste is landfilled, 3% is landfilled with energy recovery, 7% is incinerated, 2% is incinerated with energy recovery. In comparison, Switzerland only landfills 20%, Japan and Denmark 30%, France and Belgium 35%, Italy and Germany 65%.

Every day 50 million food and drink cans end up as rubbish in holes in the ground.

Each year in the UK we use enough paper to cut down a forest the size of Wales. Businesses alone discard an estimated one million tonnes of printing and writing papers a year.

Despite the prediction that it will take over one million years for a glass bottle to degrade, every day over 14 million glass bottles and jars end up as rubbish in holes in the ground.

The world's production and use of plastic materials has increased from less than 5 million tonnes in the 1950s to about 80 million tonnes today. In the UK we use around 3.5

million tonnes of plastic each year, about one-third of which is packaging. Every year 2 million sea birds die as a result of having eaten or becoming tangled up in waste plastic.

Despite the prediction that it will take around 450 years for a plastic bottle to degrade, we use more plastic (PET) bottles per capita in the UK than anywhere else in Europe while our recycling rate for plastic is only 4%.

There are growing amounts of relatively new waste, not only white goods such as fridges and cookers, but electronic goods such as computers. The rapid increase in the consumption of electronic goods, many of which have a built-in obsolescence, has resulted in vast quantities of potentially valuable materials going to landfill. In 1992 the Warren Spring Laboratory estimated that we will soon be throwing away 3 million televisions, 1 million videos, 2.5 million personal stereos, 2 million radio cassettes, 1 million home computers, 5 million telephones and 2 million microwaves every year.

• The above information is an extract from the Waste Watch web site which can be found at www.wastewatch.org.uk

© *Waste Watch*

Why does society have a problem with waste?

What does society think about waste?

Waste is a remarkably emotive topic. The noun 'waste' is loaded with negative connotations – squandering, failure and loss. The verb 'to waste' connotes feckless extravagance. The Victorians were reluctant to face up to the reality of pollution and insanitary conditions and regarded waste handling as an unspeakable occupation. This made a taboo of waste, and began a cycle that dominated legislation into the twentieth century. A problem is allowed to accumulate until a health scandal or public outburst prompts a spasm of reform. In this way, London sewerage was reformed in the nineteenth century and the Clean Air Acts did away with the lethal smog of the 1950s.

What has been the impact of the environmental movement?

The Green movement has broken the social taboo on mentioning waste and put the environment on the economic agenda. In Britain, the public now recognises that the growth of the consumer society has led to a relentless rise in poor environmental control.

Environmentalism has also underlined the world's finite resources, and that the planet's capacity to absorb our rubbish is being overloaded.

On the other hand, environmentalism offers industry new marketing opportunities. Environmental technologies, such as catalytic converters and sewage treatment systems, show how industries have kept pace with consumer demand.

What is the role of legislation?

In the UK, waste management legislation has reflected social concerns. The Environmental Protection Agency seeks to protect the whole environment – land, air and water – through the principle of 'the polluter must pay'.

It is likely that in the long term governments will use taxation to ensure that the prices of all products will reflect the environmental impact of their manufacturing process, use and ultimate disposal. Potentially, this creates a new area of competitive advantage. Producers will be able to drive down prices by minimising the volume of waste generated and ensuring that the remainder has the least environmental impact.

Effective waste strategies will become an integral part of corporate survival.

How is waste regulated?

There is a popular misconception in Britain that the waste industry is poorly regulated, but nothing could be further from the truth. The Environmental Protection Agency has imposed a strict regime on carriers and disposers, chiefly landfill operators. Anyone wishing to operate disposal, storage and treatment facilities for controlled waste must now hold a licence from the Waste Regulation Authority (WRA). WRAs supervise disposal, imposing conditions on licensees and ensuring correct practice. WRAs now check whether proposed licensees are fit and proper persons to hold a licence.

Although producers and carriers now share liability for the first time, the chief burden of liability still falls on the final disposer. Operators and owners of landfill sites will soon be responsible in perpetuity for correcting any liquid or gaseous emissions from their sites. The consequence is that landfill manage-ment is now a long-term activity where only those with financial stability should be permitted to operate.

In the United States, if a landfill operator goes bankrupt, liabilities revert back to those whose waste has entered the site during its lifetime.

There is no case law in the UK to support this practice yet, but it would seem prudent for waste producers to check the safety of the final resting place of their rubbish, otherwise it may return to haunt their balance sheet.

Most waste in the UK is subject to regulation. There are two broad categories: those that are subject to a disposal licensing regime – 'controlled wastes' – and those that are not. The second category covers waste from agriculture, mining and quarrying. Although not subject to disposal licensing, these wastes are governed by a range of policy guidelines and regulations.

The waste management industry focuses on 'controlled wastes' from industrial, domestic and commercial activities. Their disposal is governed by a unified licensing regime under the Control of Pollution Act 1974 (CoPA), now being superseded by the Environmental Protection Agency.

Within controlled wastes are a much smaller group of 'special wastes' – those that contain substances dangerous to life. Also known as 'hazardous', these are currently governed by CoPA and the Control of Pollution (Special Waste) Regulations 1980, but will very soon fall under the Environmental Protection Agency. A regulatory framework is fine for big operators, but with 3,000 other smaller companies, policing is inherently difficult.

• Reproduced by kind permission of HTI Leadership & Management. HTI is an educational charity which aims to enchance leadership and management within schools. This material was sourced from HTI's environmental educational site, which can be found at www.e4s.org.uk

© HTI

Stresses and strains

Information from the Environment Agency

Households

Households exert pressure on the environment by using energy and water, and generating waste. They consume about 30% of the energy used in the UK but, if passenger transport is included, this rises to 50%. Twenty per cent of all water supplied is consumed by households, and 5% of controlled waste is generated in the home. As consumers, we also put pressure indirectly on environmental resources, through the production of food, manufacture of goods and provision of services.

There has been a steady increase in the number of households in England and Wales since the 1970s reflecting the slight increase in population and a move to more people living alone. The number of households is projected to grow at a faster rate than the population over the next 20 years. Between 1991 and 2016, there is a projected increase in the number of households of about 4.4 million (23%) in England. This predicted increase has three basic components: population change (46%), behavioural changes (33%), and greater life expectancy (21%). Eighty per cent (3.5 million) of the total projected growth by 2016 is likely to be due to one-person households. Household growth will

be mainly in the south-west (29% increase), south-east, Cheshire, East Midlands and eastern regions, with the lowest percentage increase of 13% in Merseyside and 16% in the north-east.

The increase in the number of households is projected to contribute to the expected increase in the area of land in urban use and hence a loss to the rural environment. Some 169,000 hectares (1.3% of England's land area) are projected to change from rural uses to urban uses between 1991 and 2016, i.e. a rate of 6,800 hectares per year. By the year 2016, 11.9% of England's land is predicted to be in urban use compared with 10.6% in 1991. More households will require more energy, goods and services, and increased use of transport.

The domestic sector is one of the largest users of energy (30%). Transport consumes 32% and slightly less is used by industry (23%). Domestic energy consumption increased by 16% between 1970 and 1995, although the amount used per household has remained relatively constant and the overall growth is related to the increase in number of households. Household appliances account for about a quarter of electricity consumed in the UK. The Home Energy Conservation Act aims

to reduce carbon dioxide emissions from domestic properties by 30% by the year 2007. Local authorities are responsible for achieving this reduction.

Nearly 70% of households in England and Wales have at least one car. Twenty per cent have two cars and 4% have three or more cars. Emissions from vehicle exhausts contain nitrogen oxides, carbon dioxide, carbon monoxide, volatile organic compounds (VOC) and particulate matter. Road transport contributes three-quarters of the UK's carbon monoxide, 50% of the black smoke and nitrogen oxides, and almost 40% of the VOC emissions. Land is required for roads and the waste generated from transport includes tyres, used vehicles and vehicle components.

Direct emissions to air by households occur through the use of solid fuels, oil and gas, and use of paints and solvents. Households are responsible for 19% of the UK's black smoke emissions, 4% of carbon monoxide, 3% sulphur dioxide, 3% nitrogen dioxide and 1% of the UK's VOC emissions. But, if the emissions from power stations as a result of energy used by households are also included, households are responsible for 21% of the UK's black smoke emissions, 8% carbon monoxide,

27% sulphur dioxide, 11% nitrogen dioxide and 4% of the VOC emissions.

In England and Wales we each consume about 140 litres of water every day. Household use of water has increased significantly over time, reflecting changes in household appliances, lifestyles and expectations. In 1972 only 66% of households had washing machines, whereas this had risen to 90% by 1996. Efficient use of water is necessary to reduce or at least minimise the increasing demand for water. Toilets and baths use more than half of the water in the home. A five-minute shower instead of a bath can save an average of 55 litres of water. Heavy-duty plastic bags ('Hippos') and other devices can reduce the amount of water used to flush toilets. The use of water in the garden has also increased in recent years.

Most of the water used by households (80%) is returned to rivers or estuaries after sewage-treatment. Natural human waste contributes organic matter and nutrients such as phosphorus in sewage. Some detergents also contain phosphorus, although changing formulations have led to a decline in the 1990s. Metal and chemical products are widely used in the home. Some metals are dissolved from water pipes and solder, other substances including metals are contained in cosmetics, toiletries, medicines and domestic cleaners. Sewage-treatment normally reduces these to harmless levels but it is not always known what these harmless levels are. Recent work has suggested that even at low concentrations some substances may have a harmful effect on the environment. The use of pesticides and herbicides in gardens, misconnections from 'DIY' plumbing and misuse of road drains for oily residues create problems in fresh waters. More than 1,000 water pollution incidents in 1995 were attributed to domestic or residential premises.

Waste arising directly from households accounts for around 4 to 5% (16 to 20 million tonnes) of the waste produced annually in the UK. Each household in Britain throws

Britain's load of rubbish getting bigger and bigger

By James Meikle

Britain's throwaway society threatens to double household rubbish in 20 years as the piles mount of fast-food cartons, ready-meal packets, newspapers and even redundant computers, the government revealed yesterday.

Environment minister Michael Meacher called for a 'dramatic change of behaviour' by consumers, businesses and public bodies.

But the country could still need a near tenfold increase in incinerators to compensate for cuts in the use of council tips and landfill sites, reports published by his department suggested yesterday.

Mr Meacher revealed that only 8% of the 27m tonnes of household waste was recycled and that the home-made rubbish mountain was rising at a far faster rate. He hoped 25% could be recycled by 2005 and 30% by 2010.

Mr Meacher said local authorities could do much more to encourage roadside recycling; some were only reusing between 3% and 5% of household waste. Industry and commerce would also have to cut its waste, already running at up to 100m tonnes a year.

A draft strategy outlined yesterday warned that the number of incinerators may have to rise from about 10 to nearly 100 by 2015.

© The Guardian
July, 1999

away about one dustbin full of rubbish every week. By weight, the average dustbin contains paper and cardboard (30%), food scraps (25%), glass (10%), metals (8%), plastics (8%) and textiles, dust and other sub-stances (19%). About half of household waste could be recycled. It is estimated that only around 5% of household waste is recycled or composted in the UK. The Govern-ment has set a target for the recovery of 40% of household waste in England and Wales by 2005.

We each consume about one kilogram of meat and fish, and three kilograms of fruit and vegetables every week. The UK's self-sufficiency in food production was about 33% at the time of the First World War. In 1996, UK agriculture produced just over half (53%) of the food and animal feed consumed, and nearly 70% of the types of food which can be grown in the UK. More than three-quarters of UK land area is used for agriculture. We demand high-quality food with a long shelf-life, resulting in widespread use of chemicals in food production. Less than 1% of UK agricultural land is farmed using organic methods.

Household expenditure on recreation, entertainment and education has increased substantially since 1971, reflecting the real rise in household disposable income over the same period. Part of the increase in recreational expenditure relates to the time spent in the natural environment. Five thousand million leisure day trips were made to the countryside and coast during 1996. A quarter of all day trips were to the countryside (26%) and 3% were to the seaside or coast. Households can influence industry through their spending on goods and services. Schemes like the EU ecolabel award scheme have been set up to enable consumers to consider the environ-ment when making choices. Going for Green and the Environment Agency have developed computer software called EcoCal. EcoCal assesses an individual household's impact on the environment. Residents of the UK can obtain a copy from Going for Green by calling 0800 783 7838.

© 1998 Environment Agency

Cutting the waste we generate

Tackling waste is priority for the future, says Meacher

We must all take more responsibility for cutting the waste we generate. This means thinking not only about how we manage waste. but, more importantly, how we can use it as a resource, Environment Minister Michael Meacher said today as he published the draft waste strategy 'A Way with Waste'.

Increased recycling and energy from waste will be vital in the next decade if the country is to cut the 27 million tonnes of household waste currently produced each year. If the problem is not tackled now, on current trends household waste – increasing by 3% a year – will nearly double in 20 years. Industry and commerce must cut waste too – they now produce between 70 and 100 million tonnes a year.

The draft strategy sets goals of:
- recovering 45% of municipal waste by 2010 (recycling, composting, and incineration with energy/heat recovery);
- recycling or composting 30% of household waste by 2010.

Much of our waste comes from industry and commerce and our target is, by 2005, to reduce the amount landfilled to 85% of 1998 levels. This means that any growth has value recovered from it.

Setting out the way ahead for increased recycling, Mr Meacher said: 'We need stronger markets for recyclate. The Government's Market Development Group has now reported on this and its recommendations are published for comment today alongside this draft strategy. We will respond to these recommendations in our final strategy. Some of its recommendations are for Government itself. We will address these with vigour, seeking further views as necessary. Some are for other bodies, who will need to address these proposals equally vigorously.'

The Group's recommendations call for: a different approach to market development that focuses on new uses for recyclate and e.g. use of glass filler in asphalt roads; greater emphasis on environmental considerations, including increased demand for recycled goods and services, in public procurement decisions and private sector purchasing policies; development of improved quality and standards, through recognised specifications, good practice guidance, better public and consumer awareness, and greater emphasis on eco-design; action to stabilise the markets and reduce price volatility, including mechanism for price guarantees, the adoption of long-term contracts rather than spot prices, and a possible futures market; possible consideration of instruments to stimulate demand further.

Outlining the change in attitudes needed, Michael Meacher said: 'Our approach to municipal and industrial waste alike must change. We are determined to meet the challenges of sustainable development and of the European Directive on the landfilling of waste's stringent targets for diverting waste from landfill. To do this we must substantially increase both recycling and energy recovery.

'We have therefore set two goals by 2010 of recovering 45% of municipal waste (by recycling, composting and incineration with energy or heat recovery) and of recycling or composting 30% of household waste. To do this we must meet, as soon as possible, the existing targets of 40% recovery and 25% recycling or composting. We aim to do this by 2005.

'Beyond 2010 we must do more. By 2015 we expect to recover value from two-thirds of household waste, half of this by recycling or composting.'

Doing your bit for reducing waste

In the home . . . !

An ever-increasing demand for raw materials and vast amounts of waste has created an urgent need for waste minimisation. It has been estimated that for every tonne of household waste, another five tonnes is created at the manu-facturing stage and 20 tonnes at the site of initial extraction. Much of Britain's waste ends up in landfill sites which are becoming scarce.

Waste minimisation at the household level starts in the shop by choosing products and services with the least environmental impact.

Here are just a few examples of practical actions households can take:

- Use shredded waste paper for protective packaging
- By refillable containers for cleaners, washing solutions and detergents where possible
- Avoid disposable products such as razors, nappies, tissues etc.
- Try to buy unpackaged goods
- Reuse envelopes – purchase reuse labels
- Use a milk delivery service
- Contact the Mailing Preference Service to discourage unsolicited mailshots
- Use resealable containers for school packed lunches

For more information contact Waste Watch, the national charity promoting action on waste reduction and recycling, on their Wasteline: 0870 243 0136.

Returnable or recyclable

People are often told that it's better for the environment to buy milk and lemonade in returnable, refillable bottles, but according to INCPEN, the Industry Council for Packaging and the Environment, this advice

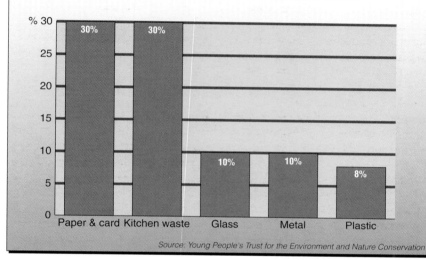

Rubbish

On average a family of four throws away about two sacks of rubbish a week, most of which could be recycled. The figures below show the main constituents of household waste

| Paper & card | Kitchen waste | Glass | Metal | Plastic |
| 30% | 30% | 10% | 10% | 8% |

Source: Young People's Trust for the Environment and Nature Conservation

can be misleading. In some instances the best choice might be to throw the bottle away rather than transport it for reprocessing or cleaning and reuse.

In other instances, refilling or recycling may be appropriate but the difference between the types of packaging and how the used packaging is handled is small compared with the environmental investment in the drink itself.

It is much more important that people do not waste the drink. Better environmental advice would be to buy the right amount.

Recycle, burn or bury?

This can't be answered because we need all three – landfill sites, incinerators and recycling schemes – and other methods of handling waste, according to INCPEN, the Industry Council for Packaging and the Environment.

Yesterday's newspaper and an empty wine bottle, provided they do not need to be transported too far, can be worth recycling and the material used again. Week-old fish skins and greasy meat trays are long past being turned into anything usable but their energy content can be put to further use if burned in a modern incinerator with energy recovery.

We also need landfill sites because all other waste treatment processes leave residues that need to be disposed of safely.

People often claim to be confused about whether recycling is a good or bad thing. Like most green issues the answer isn't simple. Recycling some things, some of the time, is good but it depends on many variable factors such as local circumstances and the type of material.

© Going For Green / Tidy Britain Group

War on waste

Information from WWF International

This is an area where everyone can make a contribution to living lightly on the planet.

Reducing the amount of waste we produce means that less ends up in already overflowing landfills; it reduces the need for new raw materials, and so helps preserve the environment from destructive processes such as mining, power generation and water exploitation. Less waste means less pollution, and reducing waste can save money! Waste can be reduced by reducing, reusing, and recycling.

Reduce

This is the most important step – if we do it well there will be less to re-use and recycle.

1. Shop carefully: buy in bulk to reduce the amount of packaging required; choose returnable or reusable containers.
2. Avoid over-packaged products and unnecessarily packaged food, e.g. cling-wrapped vegetables on polystyrene trays.
3. Choose durable articles that will last a long time.
4. Buy products with a recycled content.
5. Use rechargeable batteries where possible, cloth dishtowels and napkins instead of paper ones, and refillable ink pens. Avoid disposable plates, cups and cutlery.
6. Store food in the fridge in re-usable, airtight containers, rather than plastic cling film, tinfoil or plastic bags.
7. Take your own basket, or re-usable plastic bags, to the supermarket to avoid using new plastic shopping bags each time. Use the supermarket's trolley or basket when selecting items, and use your own bag or basket to carry it home. Ask your supermarket to take back used shopping bags.

8. In the office and at school, photocopy on both sides of the paper.

Reuse

Where possible, reuse a product several times. If you can't use it again, find someone who can.

1. Glass and plastic bottles with deposits can be returned to shops for reuse. Likewise, milk bottles are reused by distributors.
2. Wash and dry plastic bags for re-use.
3. Staple together office paper that has only been written on one side, for scrap paper.
4. Nursery schools make good use of the inside core of toilet rolls and paper towels, egg boxes, cereal boxes and jam jars.
5. Charities welcome unwanted clothes, furniture, toys, books and magazines.
6. Repair things rather than throw them away.

Recycle

If a product cannot be reused, then recycle it. The first step is to separate your waste at home into organic waste, plastic, glass, tin cans and paper – all of which can be recycled into suitable forms for reuse.

1. Glass is 100% recyclable – make use of bottle banks.
2. A compost heap is a must! Kitchen and garden waste can be added to the compost heap, or used to feed pets or garden birds.
3. There are many recycling programmes operating nation-wide.
4. Used motor oil can be handed in for recycling at your local garage.

• The above information is an extract from the WWF International web site which can be found at www.panda.org
© *The World Wide Fund For Nature*

Recycling

Information from WWF-UK

Introduction

Each year people in Britain use more than six billion drinks cans, 12 billion food cans, 1.7 million tonnes of glass, and we use an average of two trees' worth of paper each. When we are finished with them, we generally just throw them away. In 1996 almost 25 million tonnes of household waste was generated in England and Wales alone.

Happily, however, more and more people are recycling their waste – but what does recycling mean? Is it beneficial, or just a waste of time, materials and energy?

Recycling is the processing of waste or rubbish back into raw materials so that it can be made into new items. It is undoubtedly beneficial – to the individual, the community and the planet. Even so, before recycling we really need to address the problem at its root, and reduce our waste. We can, for example, buy fewer disposable items and more that have a longer lifespan. We must also learn to reuse our products – using the same bags for shopping, buying refillable items, and repairing products instead of buying replacements.

Reasons for recycling

We dump around 83 per cent of our waste in landfill sites – huge holes in the ground. But this isn't the end of the problem: poorly managed sites can cause a range of environmental problems, not least the production of methane gas, which contributes to climate change. As well as methane, a liquid called leachate is produced as the waste decomposes. This can seep into underground rivers and streams and into surface water to pollute the natural environment and cause health problems.

A further nine per cent of household waste is incinerated – but this disposal method can create pollutants such as extremely dangerous dioxins, heavy metals and the gases that cause acid rain.

Recycling waste helps avoid these problems. For example, recycling aluminium cans and foil saves 95 per cent of the energy required to produce new aluminium. Recycling these, and paper and glass, also reduces the need for raw material extraction, which often causes widespread environmental damage – and it also reduces the need for landfill space and incinerators.

What can be recycled?

A typical household dustbin contains glass, paper, card, plastic bottles, steel and aluminium cans, and bio-degradable waste such as vegetables – all of which can be recycled. Each tonne of paper recycled saves 15 average-sized trees, as well as their surrounding habitat and wildlife.

More than 20 per cent of our waste is compostable. Composting is simple and the end result improves the quality of the soil without using chemical fertilisers, peat or commercially produced compost.

Glass is one of the most easily recyclable materials. In the UK our record is poor, but improving: we now recycle 29 per cent (500,000 tonnes) collected from around 17,000 bottle banks nationwide, compared with 15 per cent only a few years ago. Even so, we still have a long way to go: the Dutch, for example, recycle over 75 per cent of their glass.

Only glass bottles and containers – nothing else – should

A typical household dustbin contains glass, paper, card, plastic bottles, steel and aluminium cans, and bio-degradable waste such as vegetables – all of which can be recycled

---

be put in a bottle bank. And just as important is sorting by colour: putting the wrong coloured glass, or other kinds such as window glass, light bulbs or kitchenware, will contaminate the entire batch. And contaminated batches usually end up in landfill sites.

An estimated 100 million tonnes of *plastic* are produced worldwide every year, accounting for four per cent of oil consumption. Harmful toxic chemicals are used in some plastics to make them flexible and to stop discolouration and cracking. These substances can leach from the containers into the products they are holding.

A great deal of plastic is used for packaging. Because it degrades extremely slowly, it causes all sorts of disposal problems – it's well known that many birds, fish and small mammals are killed when they get trapped in drinks can plastic holders.

It is best not to buy disposable plastic products or anything that comes with plastic packaging in the first place. But reuse whatever plastic containers you have for storing household items – though not food – and always reuse plastic carrier bags. Some retailers such as The Body Shop refill their plastic cosmetics containers – and with new regulations encouraging large producers and retailers to recycle their waste, many more outlets may soon be offering similar services.

Plastic recycling schemes are slowly becoming available, so do use them. Your old plastic can end up becoming drain pipes, fence posts, telephones – or even fleece jumpers.

Baked bean cans, cars and refrigerators all have one thing in common: they are made from *ferrous metals* – in other words, they contain iron. Around nine million tonnes of ferrous material is recycled every year – a large amount coming from old cars.

Products made from *non-ferrous* metals are non-magnetic and include aluminium cans and foil. Every year in the UK, we use more than six billion drinks cans – the vast majority of which end up in landfill sites. Both steel and aluminium cans have a value and should be recycled (some charities have set up local schemes for this). Many food and drinks cans now display a symbol telling you what they are made of – and if they don't, a magnet will tell you: steel will cling to it.

Remember, too, that mining for aluminium can be very harmful to the environment: another reason why it makes sense to reuse or recycle. When doing so, don't forget to rinse out the cans and crush them first.

Textiles can be recycled by taking them to a local charity shop, where they will either be passed on to those in need, or sold to aid further work.

Furniture is easily recyclable. Charities such as the Salvation Army will accept it in good condition, and there may also be a local scheme that will collect on request.

Garden tools can be reused. Tools for Self Reliance sends old or unused hand tools to agricultural communities in the developing world.

White goods. Old refrigerators and freezers need to be disposed of with great care because most contain CFCs which do great damage to the ozone layer. It is now possible to remove and recycle CFCs, and most local authorities collect white goods, including old washing machines. Contact your local council's Recycling Officer or the Waste Watch Wasteline who can tell you the nearest CFC recycling site.

Other goods. Many small companies specialise in the repair and resale of broken radio or television equipment and will normally pay you for the item. Or you could donate any unwanted working equipment to schools or charities. It is now even possible to recycle personal computers beyond repair. Simply enquiring about such schemes can encourage other companies to set them up.

Batteries require more than 35 times more energy to make than they produce. They also cause significant problems for the environment when they are thrown away because of the toxic and poisonous substances they contain. Wherever possible, we should avoid them altogether and opt for rechargeable batteries as a last resort. Rechargeable and non-rechargeable recycling schemes are beginning to emerge, so it's worth contacting the manufacturer for details.

Car batteries are a particular problem because they contain large quantities of hazardous waste such as lead and acid.

If you need to dispose of *hazardous waste* such as car batteries, garden chemicals, herbicides, pesticides, paint, solvents such as white spirit or paint thinners, brake fluid or oil, contact your local council, who will advise you what to do. Remember that it is illegal to pour engine oil down the drain, and with very good reason – a gallon of oil has the potential to pollute up to a million gallons of water.

Some DIY stores are now offering recycling schemes for a few of these items.

We can all help recycle

Recycling needs to become second nature to us in everything we do. Companies can help by designing more environmentally-friendly and recycled goods, and keeping packaging to a minimum. The government also has an important role in controlling the disposal of waste and providing support for both industry and local authorities to start up recycling schemes.

Always try to buy recycled products – but be cautious of products with broad environmental claims because there may be little evidence to back them up. In the case of paper, look for the highest content of post-consumer recycled paper. And look for wood products bearing the Forest Stewardship Council logo which tells you that the wood comes from a sustainable source.

Further action

If you would like more information about how to minimise your environmental impact, contact Global Action Plan. In partnership with WWF, GAP runs the Action at Home programme which helps people to take effective environmental action in their home, workplace and community. The programme, which runs for six months, provides monthly action packs on waste, shopping, transport, water, energy and 'next steps'. Already, more than 14,000 households have taken part in Action at Home – and not least among their achievements was an average 25 per cent reduction in waste.

And finally . . .

Recycling is not a new idea. Since life began, one species' waste has been used by another as a resource. This is known as the 'closed resource loop' of natural ecosystems and we are mimicking this whenever we re-use or recycle our waste. The good news is that by disposing of our waste with care, we can begin to move closer to the day when we are living in balance with the natural world.

• Text prepared by Stephen Waygood, WWF Environmental Management Officer

What is recycling?

Information from Going For Green and Waste Watch

Recycling means using things that have already been used, to make new things. It also includes reusing things as they are, and giving things you no longer need to other people to use.

Some things which are recycled:

- Glass bottles and jars can be melted down and made into new glass bottles and jars.
- Milk bottles are used up to twenty times.
- Cans can be melted down and made into new cans.
- Paper can be soaked to turn it back into pulp.
- Then the paper fibres can be made into new paper.
- Scrap paper and card can be used for notes and lists.

Some things which can be passed on:

Toys, clothes and books can be given to jumble sales and charity shops. Furniture can be sold or given to other people.

Make a notepad out of some scrap paper.

- Use a piece of card to make a firm base.
- Cut up some paper that has been used (printed on one side).
- Glue or staple the paper to the card.

- Then put it by the telephone for messages.
- List the things that could be recycled from your home.

Could we recycle more of our waste?

Probably over half the things we throw away could be recycled. That means we could recycle 10 times as much as we do now.

Some reasons why we do not recycle more are:

- Recycling needs a lot of organisation and special equipment in the home.
- There is the idea that there are difficulties in recycling some materials, particularly plastics: this is not the case as all three types of plastic can be recycled when sites are available. If plastic recycling facilities are not available ask an adult to contact your local authority to see if they have plans to provide sites.
- There must be uses for the recycled material. Someone must want to buy it and use it to make new things which they can sell.
- See if your local supermarket or shop sells any of the following:
  A. Tissues, toilet paper or kitchen roll made from recycled paper.
  B. Dustbin bags or kitchen bin bags made from recycled plastic.

- If it does, ask whoever does the shopping in your house to consider buying them instead of items that are not made from recycled material.

How can I help to make sure more of our waste is reused or recycled?

We all help to create waste, so everyone needs to help to cut down how much is thrown away. As well as things already suggested you might like to consider some of these activities:

- Involve your friends in doing the actions in this article.
- Join with your friends to collect cans and bottles for recycling.
- Make a poster about reusing and recycling waste, and ask if it can be displayed in your school, community centre, local shop or doctor's waiting room.
- Pass on clothes and toys which you no longer need to a jumble sale or charity shop.
- Ask your school or group to have 'collection weeks'.

Why should we bother to reuse and recycle some things?

The most important reasons for not throwing things away are:

- Making things from recycled material can use less energy and cause less pollution.

What is recycled?

In Britain we recycle in one year:

1 out of 3 newspapers

1 out of 4 glass bottles and jars

1 out of 4 items of clothing

1 out of 3 metal drinks cans

1 out of 25 plastic bottles

Source: Going for Green/Waste Watch

- Less space is needed to get rid of waste.
- Less new material is needed to make things.
- Many people do not like wasting things and would prefer them to be recycled.
- Making aluminium cans from old ones uses only one-twentieth of the energy that is needed to make them from raw materials.

With the help of an adult, group leader or older brother/sister:
- Design a poster (on recycled paper) to put on your kitchen wall to encourage all the people in your family to recycle and reuse more things.
- Make a list of some ways of using waste material to replace things you might buy, such as using yoghurt pots for plant seedlings, or clear plastic egg boxes as little jelly moulds.
- Then have a go at one of them.

What things are recycled?

The main things that can be recycled are: glass bottles and jars; food and drinks cans; aluminium foil; newspapers; magazines; clothes and other textiles; plastic bottles. However, only some of these things are recycled.

We recycle in Britain in one year:
- 1 out of 3 newspapers
- 1 out of 4 glass bottles and jars
- 1 out of 4 items of clothing
- 1 out of 3 metal drinks cans
- 1 out of 25 plastic bottles

With the help of an adult, group leader or older brother/sister:
- Find out if there are, and make a list of, recycling banks, with locations, in your area for bottles and jars, cans, textiles, plastics and paper. Circulate it to your friends and their parents so they can use them.
- With the help of a grown-up, work out how to take these things to the recycling banks, instead of putting them in your dustbin.

• The above information is an extract from *Waste Month – Rubbish Rules*, a leaflet produced by Going for Green and Waste Watch. See page 41 for their address details.

© *Going for Green and Waste Watch*

Rubbish rebate aims to reward recyclers

By Anthony Barnett

Britain is creating too much rubbish and running out of places to dispose of it. To add to the problem, the British have one of the worst recycling records in Europe.

A survey published tomorrow by the environmental organisation Waste Watch will show that while nine out of 10 people claim to recycle rubbish, only 6 per cent of Britain's domestic waste is actually recycled – compared with 42 per cent in Switzerland, 34 per cent in Germany and 36 per cent in the Netherlands. The United States recycles three times as much rubbish as the UK.

Britain's homes currently produce 26 million tonnes of domestic waste a year, 30 per cent up on five years ago.

The Government is drafting a Green Paper on a waste strategy for the next 25 years. Among the drastic solutions being considered is a 'rubbish' rebate, whereby householders who recycle more rubbish pay less council tax.

Pilot studies involving dustcarts that can weigh and keep a record of each household's rubbish are being planned. Similar schemes operate in Germany and the US and can greatly reduce the volume of waste.

A Government study suggests that variable charging, which takes into account the proportion of a household's recycled rubbish, would lead to the average household being charged about £71 a year, with less than £33 for the poorest and about £116 for the richest households, which are likely to generate far more rubbish.

Waste Watch, citing an NOP opinion poll, reports that 57 per cent of the public would support proposals for variable charging.

© *The Guardian*
February, 1999

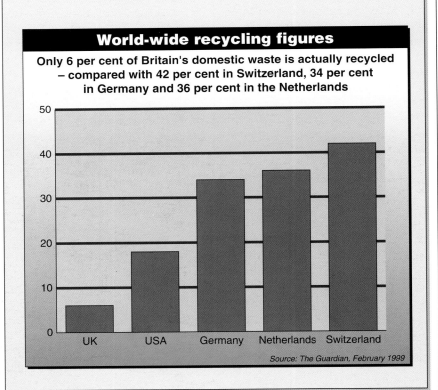

World-wide recycling figures

Only 6 per cent of Britain's domestic waste is actually recycled – compared with 42 per cent in Switzerland, 34 per cent in Germany and 36 per cent in the Netherlands

Source: The Guardian, February 1999

Recycling – the facts

Information from the Pulp and Paper Information Centre

Recycling is one of those rare activities from which practically everyone derives a benefit. The paper industry is a recycler *par excellence* – and has been for hundreds of years. Before woodpulp became his major raw material, the papermaker used old rags. Today, although some rags are still used, by far the largest material for recycling is paper and board itself. Papermakers are therefore understandably aggrieved when, as a result of widespread misunderstandings in the public mind, custard pies in the face rather than bouquets in the hand tend to be the order of the day. The misconceptions are not limited to the industry's record in recycling: its use of wood is the basis of even more confused thinking and public misstatement. Waste paper represents over 60% of the fibre used to manufacture paper and board in the UK and because only 9% of the industry's fibre needs are derived from UK timber, waste paper is seen as the industry's 'urban forest'.

The pulp and paper industry is split into several distinct product sectors, some of which use a lot more waste paper than others. In 1998 the printings and writings sector used approximately 18% recycled fibre, UK newsprint manufacturers used over 94% waste paper in their production and corrugated case manufacturers use on average 105% waste in its manufacture (there is some weight loss due to staples and glues, binding etc.).

Over the last ten years more than £2 billion has been invested in plant to recover and reuse waste paper as a source of fibre for papermaking. As a result of that investment consumption of waste paper and board (as a source of wood fibre) has increased from 2 million tonnes to 4.7 million tonnes.

How do you perceive recycling? Do you just think of it as being the paper bank in the car park behind the local supermarket? Or a doorstep collection once every now and then on behalf of a local charity? Recycling is not a new concept – it is as old as 'paper' itself. Paper as we know it today originates from old clothes, using the cotton, hemp and flax – genuine recycling before it became fashionable!

The Victorians knew all about recycling and indeed were highly organised – with street finders (young children were used), sewer hunters, dredger and river finders and mudlarks – young waifs and strays who collected any flotsam and jetsam to make a few pennies. There were even specialist finders of cigar ends, wood and 'pure' (dog dung which was worth 2d-3d a pail. This was used in the leather tanning business).

The list goes on – buyers of clothes, rags, metals, grease, even dripping and animal skins such as hares and rabbits. The markets were full of street sellers of all manner of second-hand articles, weapons and curiosities. In the 1850s the refuse of leavings of one class of people really provided a livelihood for the class immediately below it.

Despite all the effort involved we are still consuming and throwing away around 3 million tonnes of paper and board. Paper contains wood fibre from trees, so what constructive action can be taken to utilise the natural resource again rather than just throwing it away? The industry's use of recovered paper has risen steadily for the last 14 years.

The packaging sector is a major use of waste paper which represents 95% of the fibre used in the UK manufacture of packaging papers and boards. Packaging grades are able to effectively utilise lower grades of waste paper such as newspapers, cartons and corrugated boxes.

Waste paper cannot be recycled indefinitely as strength is lost every time the fibre is recycled. A constant supply of new fibres is therefore essential to maintain the papermaking chain. Almost 100% waste paper is used in the UK manufacture of corrugated case materials, but this excellent record is dependent upon

the introduction of new kraft fibres. Much of the wood used is either from waste from sawmills or thinnings taken from the forest to allow the remaining trees to grow to healthy maturity.

How to recycle

Paper, what would we do without it?

A life without paper is almost impossible to imagine. We write on it, read from it, wrap presents in it, package our food in it, decorate our homes with it – the list is endless. Find out what you can do to recycle your waste paper.

Why recycle?

In the UK today, nearly 5 million tonnes of paper is being dumped in landfill or incinerated each year. This is a valuable raw material that can be reused to create new paper and board products. Waste paper is a raw material upon which the UK paper industry relies.

What can be recycled?

Almost any household waste paper can be recycled, including used newspapers, cardboard, packaging, stationery, 'direct mail', magazines, catalogues, greeting cards and wrapping paper. It is important that these papers are kept separate from other household waste – contaminated papers are not acceptable for recycling.

Collections

Get in touch with the Recycling Officer at your Local Authority who will be able to provide details of any collection schemes they run. Many Local Authorities operate systems such as kerbside collection schemes. These usually operate by asking you to leave your waste on the kerbside on specified dates. It is then collected for recycling.

Waste paper banks

You can take your waste paper to a local waste paper bank which can be found in a range of sites, including supermarkets, car parks, schools, and civic amenity centres. Your Local Authority should be able to provide details of where these are in your area.

There are three main types of waste paper: white, newspapers and magazines, and packaging. Notices displayed on the banks will tell you what sort of paper is acceptable.

If you are using a car, include a visit to the paper bank during a journey which you are already planning – recycling is easy and effective if it is convenient.

Community groups

You can turn your waste paper into a charitable donation by giving it to a local community group for recycling. A volunteer may collect the paper from you to help boost their funds.

Many Local Authorities pass on Recycling Credits to small groups who collect domestic waste for recycling. Many schools, charities and community groups benefit from these Credits through receiving money for every tonne of waste paper they collect. This can be a bonus for fund raising. If you belong to a local community group contact your Recycling Officer for further details.

© Pulp and Paper Information Centre
January, 2000

Britain fails to hit recycling target

The Government was forced to admit yesterday that it had failed to meet the target, set a decade ago, of recycling a quarter of the domestic dustbin by 2000.

The best estimate of the amount of the dustbin recycled in 1999 is nine per cent, some 16 percentage points short of the target set in 1990, Michael Meacher, the environment minister, admitted yesterday. Mr Meacher said it was 'perfectly clear' from when Labour took office that the target of recycling 25 per cent of the average dustbin, set by a Tory Environment Secretary, Chris Patten, would not be met because not enough had been done to make it happen.

The recycling rate has increased from 2.9 per cent in 1989-90 but remains one of the lowest in Europe. Meanwhile the amount of domestic

By Charles Clover,
Environment Editor

rubbish, about 28 million tonnes, has been growing at three per cent a year. Mr Meacher said there was a 'great risk' of Britain failing to meet the legally-binding EU target of recovering 50 per cent of all packaging – bottles, cans and paper – by 2002, and could face prosecution in the European Court.

The recycling rate has increased from 2.9 per cent in 1989-90 but remains one of the lowest in Europe

Britain is entering a period in which several legally-enforceable targets come into force. The EU landfill directive requires a 25 per cent cut by 2005 in waste going to landfill sites. Meeting the target would require 'an absolute revolution', said Mr Meacher.

Jeff Cooper, of the Environment Agency, which is responsible for carrying out waste policy, said: 'The 25 per cent recycling target was set in mysterious circumstances and without an environmental justification.' Incineration with energy recovery was a better option than recycling for some materials, he said. Mike Childs, of Friends of the Earth, said: 'People can't recycle enough because they don't have decent facilities.'

© Telegraph Group Limited,
London 2000

What can we recycle?

Information from Waste Watch

Material for recycling needs to be clean and uncontaminated, which means that problems are caused when the wrong materials are put into the wrong recycling banks. Don't deposit mixed material or material that is dirty. Make sure that you wash bottles and cans in left-over washing-up water (running the hot water specially is a waste of water and energy!). Always put the correct materials in the correct recycling bank. Technology is developing that will be able to deal with more mixed and contaminated material, however at present we need to take care in order for recycling to be efficient.

Glass

Bottle banks are found in many local council areas and are divided into those accepting clear, green and brown glass. Blue glass can be put into the green bank, and clear glass with coloured coatings can be put into the clear bank as the coating will burn off. The labels on bottles and jars will be removed during the recycling process, however remove as many plastic or metal rings and tops as possible. Only recycle bottles and jars – never lightbulbs, sheet glass or Pyrex-type dishes as these are made from a different type of glass.

Paper

Most local authorities have recycling banks for newspapers and magazines, as this is the most abundant type of paper in household waste. Make sure that you don't put other types of paper in, such as cardboard or junk mail, as this will contaminate the load and the reprocessors will not accept it. Some local authorities may have separate banks for these. Packaging such as milk and juice cartons cannot be recycled as paper as they have a plastic lining which would contaminate the process.

Aluminium and steel cans

Many local authorities have mixed can banks accepting both aluminium and steel cans, although some have aluminium-only banks as uncontaminated aluminium has a higher value. Aluminium can be recognised by the fact that it does not stick to a magnet, has a very shiny silver base and is very light in weight. Steel cans are also called 'tins' as they contain a very thin layer of tin. Try to crush drinks cans before recycling, either with a can crusher or by squashing them underfoot. Aerosol cans made from steel or aluminium can be recycled in Save-a-can banks (check the front of the banks for guidance), but they must be empty and should not be crushed.

Textiles

Charities such as Oxfam and Scope run textiles banks for unwanted clothing, which are then sold in charity shops, given to the homeless or sent abroad. Even damaged or unwearable clothing can be converted into items such as wiping cloths, shredded for use as filling for items such as furniture or car insulation, or rewoven into new yarn or fabric. If you deposit shoes, tie them together as they tend to go astray!

Plastic

Plastic is a difficult material to recycle as there are many different types of plastic (often indicated by a number, or letters such as PP, PET or PVC). The variation in plastic means that different reprocessing techniques are required. The different types of plastic therefore need to be collected separately, or sorted after collection, as reprocessors will specify which type of plastic they will accept. Plastic in household waste is often food packaging and therefore too contaminated to be recycled effectively.

Plastic is a light, bulky part of household waste, and therefore it is difficult for councils to store and transport sufficient quantities of plastic to make recycling economically viable. Many councils have found it to be too expensive and do not have facilities for plastic at all, while others recycle only plastic bottles which are worth more money. If your council does not recycle plastic, you could try putting pressure on them to start doing so, but meanwhile try to reduce your usage and reuse as much plastic as possible. If your council does recycle plastic, make sure that you are recycling the right

type of plastic, and always remove the tops of plastic containers so that they can be crushed.

Organic waste

Organic household waste is food and garden waste. Organic waste is a problem if sent to landfill, because it is impossible to separate out from other waste once mingled, and will rot, producing methane, a greenhouse gas responsible for global warming. The best use of organic waste is either to compost it through a centralised composting scheme run by your council, or to compost it at home. Find out if your council has facilities for taking garden waste for composting, or you may be able to separate kitchen waste for a kerbside collection scheme if one exists in your area. Alternatively, build or invest in a home composter for the garden, or try a worm bin for indoor use! Check to see if your council supplies reduced-cost recycling bins.

Electrical and electronic equipment

There are very few facilities for recycling household electrical or electronic waste. British Telecom telephones can be returned and there is a scheme for recycling certain types of mobile phone. There are a number of schemes for repairing and recycling goods such as refrigerators and washing machines which can then be passed on to low-income house-holds, and some charity shops may take old electrical equipment that is still working. Call the Waste Watch Wasteline on 0870 243 0136 for details of schemes in your area. Check with your council to see if they have facilities for household appliances, electronic equipment, or CFC extraction for old refrigerators. You can arrange for the council to remove bulky household items for disposal.

Batteries

There are currently no facilities for recycling ordinary household batteries in the UK. Batteries are varied and complex, come in different shapes and types, and are consequently very difficult to sort and recycle. The toxic materials have now been removed from ordinary batteries and they are safe to dispose of with your normal household waste. Rechargeable batteries, or nickel cadmium batteries, do still contain hazardous metals and should be returned to the manufacturer where possible. A few local authorities provide facilities for recycling these, as well as lead acid car batteries, which may also be returned to garages. If you use rechargeable batteries, look out for the new versions containing no mercury or cadmium, e.g. rechargeable alkaline manganese (RAM) batteries.

Furniture

A network of furniture projects exists across the UK consisting of small-scale local projects who take old household furniture and pass it on to community groups, low-income families and other groups in need. Call the Wasteline for further details. Contact your council to dispose of broken bulky household waste.

Hazardous waste

Household hazardous waste such as paint, solvents and garden chemicals comes under the jurisdiction of your local council. Take it to a civic amenity site if facilities exist, or contact your council. Some councils also provide facilities for de-gassing fridges and for recycling fluorescent tubes.

Mixed packaging

Packaging is often made up of a mixture of materials, such as 'tetra paks' which can be made up of paper, plastic and metal, making recycling difficult. There is a lack of facilities and technology for recycling mixed packaging, meaning that the materials are difficult to separate out without contamination.

Packaging is a very visible form of waste, making up around one-third of the average household dustbin. Packaging is often necessary to protect the product, to prolong its lifespan and to provide essential information. However, over-packaging does occur, especially for marketing purposes. Basic foods such as bread and rice are rarely overpackaged, while convenience foods often have two or three layers of packaging. Try to avoid overpackaging where possible, and when choosing a product, pick the packaging material which is easiest for you to recycle locally.

The recycling symbol

Products and packaging often have some kind of recycling symbol on them. The most common is the mobius loop, which can mean that a product is either recyclable or has some recycled content. Unless the product states the percentage of recycled content, the symbol usually means that the product can be recycled. However, this does not mean that it will be recycled, or that such facilities exist. Many products can be recycled in theory, but the technology may not be available to provide collection schemes for householders.

Check that a product:
1) contains a high percentage of post-consumer waste, and
2) is made from a material which you can easily recycle in your local area.

Send off for our *Buy Recycled* information sheet for more details on labelling.

Make your voice heard !

Remember that you have the power to change things both as a consumer and as a voter, so speak up! If your council does not recycle plastic bottles or provide home compost bins, contact them and ask them why. If packaging has the recyclable symbol on it, but you cannot find a facility to recycle it, write to the manufacturer and ask them if one exists. Put pressure on shops and supermarkets to stock recycled products. Remember that you can make a difference!

Why not set up your own recycling project? Wasteline information sheets contain advice on setting up collection schemes for individual materials, or ask about our publication *Community Recycling*, a step-by-step practical guide for people wanting to set up or expand a community recycling project in their area.

• The above information is an extract from the Waste Watch web site which can be found at www.wastewatch.org.uk
© Waste Watch

Buy recycled – an introduction

Information from the National Recycling Forum

Reduce, rethink, recycle and buy recycled

Choosing and buying recycled products is part of an overall waste reduction strategy. Source reduction is an issue that often gets overlooked.

Possible activities include:

- Cut down on overpackaged products – is packaging reusable?
- Purchase refillable or reusable products, e.g. printer or toner cartridges
- Use or lease equipment that has waste reduction features, e.g. photocopiers, email etc.
- Use durable items where relevant, not one-trip disposable items
- Buy equipment that can easily be mended, or has interchangeable parts
- Specify/buy items made with recycled materials
- Check stationery supplier catalogues for recycled items
- Consider using cost savings from waste reduction activities, e.g. photocopiers set to double-sided, to pay for activities that may cost a little more until economies of scale kick in
- Investigate the options for centralised purchasing between departments or even between organisations. Bulk buying cuts costs and gives you more negotiating power with your supplier

Barriers and opportunities to buying recycled

There are both market and policy issues to overcome. Perceived or real constraints to buying recycled include:

- Cost, quality and availability
- Understanding what is a 'recycled' product
- The plethora of labels and conflicting or misleading information
- Locating suppliers
- Perceived or real operational difficulties in using recycled materials
- Pursuing the best environmental option – how to increase the utilisation of post-consumer materials

Resistance to innovation and reluctance to alter corporate purchasing practices is a key barrier facing both product manufacturers and the more open-minded buyers and product specifiers in public and private sectors. There is an increasing range of recycled products in the marketplace, usually meeting or exceeding demands of quality, availability and reliability. New technologies and operational practices to accommodate recycled content materials exist now. The barriers lie in finding ways of increasing public awareness and confidence in recycled content products to encourage greater take-up in the specification, tendering and purchasing process.

Myths and reality

Myth: Recycled products are poor quality.

Reality: False. Aluminium and glass can be recycled repeatedly without a loss in quality. Paper does suffer a reduction in quality as paper fibres shorten with each reprocessing which limits the number of times it can be recycled. But high-quality paper is readily available and lower grades of paper

are suitable for many uses. Throughout the world, military and commercial aircraft use retread tyres, as do time-critical courier services such as Federal Express.

Myth: Recycled products are too expensive.
Reality: Recycled products should not cost more but for some product areas economies of scale do result in higher prices. That is why creating consumer demand is so important. It can help lower prices.

Myth: Recycled products are not attractive.
Reality: Gone are the days of grey and grainy recycled paper. For many items it is impossible to distinguish between recycled and non-recycled items.

Myth: The product range is too small and hard to find.
Reality: Recycled products are increasingly found in everyday retail outlets, specialist stores and in business supplies catalogues.

Myth: Recycled products consume more energy and resources than a product made from primary materials.
Reality: False. Many recycled materials offer significant savings in terms of energy and water as well as reductions in resource use. For example, manufacturing 1 tonne of recycled paper results in 74% less air pollution and 34% less water pollution than manufacturing a tonne of paper from virgin wood pulp. There are an increasing number of opportunities to substitute recycled material for virgin or to incorporate a greater amount of post-consumer materials.

Negative experience in the past with recycled products re-inforces the inertia. The view that 'we have always bought that product, so why change now?' is commonly expressed. Combating these myths and prejudices takes time and leadership but change can be accelerated through the provision of accurate information, good practice case studies, demonstration projects and a supportive national framework.

• The above is an extract from the National Recycling Forum web site which can be found at www.nrf.org.uk

© *National Recycling Forum*

Make the pledge to buy recycled!

Information from Going for Green and the Tidy Britain Group

Recycled products are becoming increasingly popular with consumers and a major campaign this October will give shoppers an opportunity to tell the supermarkets what recycled goods they want to buy.

Pledge cards will be available in many of the major supermarkets for shoppers to sign and give their views. In addition to this, local authority recycling officers up and down the country will be organising events to support the campaign.

The buy recycled campaign aims to encourage people to recycle more rubbish and then to buy more products and packaging made from recycled materials. Organised by the Local Authority Recycling Advisory Committee (LARAC), the campaign is the first of its kind to unite partners in central and local government, retail, manufacturing and waste management to drive home the waste awareness message.

Although, in the past, recycled products have suffered from an image problem, this is not the case today. Now, for many goods, the fact that they are made from

recycled material is a selling point. These include:

• Steel and aluminium cans, paper products such as egg cartons, greetings cards, gift-wrapping paper, tissues and toiler paper and padded mailbags.
• Plastic products such as refuse sacks, carrier bags, compost bins, garden furniture, street furniture, pallets, plant pots, toner cartridges, fleece jackets and sleeping-bag filling.

Many recycled products and packaging will soon be displaying the buy recycled logo to show that they are made from recycled materials. Companies permitted to use the logo produce a range of goods from plastic carrier bags to tyres.

• The above information was produced by Going for Green and the Tidy Britain Group. See page 41 for address details.

© *Going For Green / Tidy Britain Group*

Understanding terminology

Information from the National Recycling Forum

The meaning of terms commonly used in connection with recycling and recycled content products are given below. However, it should be pointed out that these are not necessarily universally agreed and other definitions may be used in different contexts.

Closing the loop
The process of recycling is not complete until collected recyclable materials have been reprocessed, manufactured into new products and those products bought by consumers, including industry.

Contaminant
Any material harmful to the recycling process when included with recyclable material.

Economic instruments
A tool with the intention of ensuring that all environmental costs are paid ('internalise the externalities'). Waste-related economic instruments include: product charges, collection charges, disposal charges, emission charges, and deposit-refund systems.

Grade
A class of secondary material that is distinguished from similar classes on the basis of quality, appearance, use, content, density or other factors.

Groundwood papers
A category of papers made by grinding wood mechanically producing a 'low-grade' sheet. Newspaper and telephone books are examples of groundwood paper.

High-grade waste paper
Waste paper with the most value, consisting of pulp substitute and de-inking high grade categories.

Low-grade waste paper
Commonly referred to as bulk grades, usually of lesser value, consists of newspaper, corrugated and mixed paper.

Market development
The United States' Environmental Protection Agency (EPA) defines this as the process of strengthening or expanding both intermediate and end-uses of materials collected for reuse or recycling.

Mill broke
Waste generated within the paper-making process (normally returned to the process).

Pre-consumer materials
Production wastes or factory scrap generated by manufacturers and product converters, for example trimmings, damaged or obsolete goods, and overruns. Uncontaminated with other materials, they can be fed straight back into the production system, resulting in high-quality goods. Plastics and steel shavings are routinely recycled in this manner. Alternative terms in regular use are: post-industrial waste or industrial waste, process scrap, and manufacturing waste, with different industries tending to use different terms.

Post-consumer materials
A finished product or other material that has served its intended use and has been discarded for disposal or recovery, having completed its life as a consumer item. Post-consumer materials do not include those materials and by-products generated from, and commonly reused within, an original manufacturing process. (US EPA 1993).

Post-use
With particular reference to plastic, this is defined as 'Materials collected from outside the individual manufacturing industry after it has been used for its primary purpose. This can include material from agricultural use, commercial, industrial, retailing, distribution and domestic outlets, but in all cases the material will have been used for the purpose for which was manufactured' (British Polythene Industries 1994).

Pulp substitutes
Unprinted, clean waste paper that can be used directly in papermaking as a substitute for wood pulp.

Recovered materials
This is a broad term, covering both 'pre-consumer' and 'post-consumer' materials which would otherwise be regarded as 'waste'.

Recycling
The collection and separation of materials from the waste stream and subsequent processing to produce marketable products. Recycling differs from product reuse because of the need to process the recovered material to realise its value. At its core, recycling is about shifting to an environmentally responsible manufacturing economy that conserves natural resources, energy and disposal capacity. The most desirable form of recycling, environmentally and economically, is when the recycling process creates products that are of comparable, or only slightly lowered, quality to the original. Energy savings are often quite significant in this

high-grade recycling. An example is aluminium, which can be recycled again and again without losing any of its properties. Glass is another example. Some materials, notably paper, do suffer a loss of quality on being recycled, and this limits the number of times recycling can occur. However there are many applications that do not require a high-quality, bleached white paper product, for example toilet tissue and paper towels.

Recyclable

This is a term often used loosely, and sometimes misleadingly, on products. For example, just because a product is 'recyclable' does not mean it is environmentally benign. Most products have some environmental impact when the entire lifespan is taken into consideration. Even if a product is technically 'recyclable', collection facilities may not exist in a particular locality.

Recycled content

The term 'recycled' does not mean that a product contains 100% recovered materials. Nor does it mean that a product contains post-consumer materials. Recycled means that a product contains some recovered materials. 'Recycled content' can vary from small percentages of pre-consumer to 100% post-consumer materials.

Recycled feedstock

Material that has been recovered from the waste stream and is suitable for manufacturing new products.

Remanufacturing

A process of refurbishing a manufactured article in order to extend its lifespan. The term is frequently used for toner cartridges for photocopiers and laser printers whereby the original cartridge is checked for wear, parts replaced if necessary, and refilled for further use.

Reuse

Reuse of containers and/or packaging in the original form, either by householders, or via the manufacturer, without reprocessing.

Secondary material

Recyclable materials such as waste paper and scrap metals.

Source reduction

Waste prevention actions taken close to the source of waste generation, i.e. the point at which changed behaviour or direct action can reduce the volume of waste generated that would otherwise be recycled, incinerated or dumped in landfills. Source reduction is therefore an approach that precedes waste management by addressing how products are manufactured, purchased and used. Without waste prevention, everything else can only ever be a second-best option.

Source separation

The separation of individual secondary materials at the point of generation for recycling.

Sustainable consumption

The United Nations Environment Programme's Oslo Symposium 1994 used the following working definition, 'the use of goods and services that respond to basic needs and bring a better quality of life, while minimising the use of natural resources, toxic materials and emissions of waste and pollutants over the life cycle, so as not to jeopardise the needs of future generations'.

Waste

Any substance or object which the holder discards or intends or is required to discard is considered as waste (EU Directive 75/442).

• The above is an extract from the National Recycling Forum web site which can be found at www.nrf.org.uk

© National Recycling Forum

Is your rubbish rubbish?

Not everything you throw out this week will be rubbish

Consider these facts:
- Producing new aluminium cans from used cans saves up to 95% of the energy needed to produce cans from raw materials.
- Every tonne of glass recycled saves over one tonne of raw materials like sand and limestone. This means less quarrying, less damage to our countryside, less pollution, valuable energy savings and less global warming.

Here are some top tips:
- Use your council's recycling scheme, if they have one.
- When you are going to the supermarket, make use of the recyling banks provided.
- Why not compost your garden and appropriate food waste?

Reducing rubbish is not just about recycling. You can also:
- Buy products with less packaging.
- Reuse items such as bottles, carrier bags and refillable containers.

And, protect your local environment:
- Bin your litter.
- Dispose of chemicals or oil in local authority facilities.
- Don't dump waste in water or on the ground.
- Don't try to flush away items such as nappies, condoms, or cotton buds. Bag it and bin it.

Doing your bit is easy.

© Department for the Environment, Transport and the Regions (DETR), Crown Copyright

Materials for packaging

Information from the Industry Council for Packaging and the Environment (INCPEN)

Plastics

We use plastics in nearly everything we do, often without realising it. At home, clothes, carpets, baths and brushes are often made of plastics. So too are parts of fridges and freezers, vacuum cleaners and washing machines. Modern houses have plastic guttering and downpipes; the connections to water and gas mains are made of plastic piping. Electrical wiring is insulated with a plastic covering.

Heart valves and false teeth are made of plastics. So are records and video tapes, compact discs and camera film. More than a thousand plastic parts are built into the average European car.

Where do plastics come from?

The first plastic, celluloid, was made from coal and was used in the manufacture of billiard balls to avoid using ivory from elephants' tusks. Nowadays, only table tennis balls are made from celluloid.

Only 4% of the oil consumed in this country is used to make plastics and less than half of this is used to make plastics for packaging.

Plastics for packaging

Packaging plastics are produced in chemical factories and have rather long names. The six major ones are:
LDPE – Low density polyethylene
HDPE – High density polyethylene
PP – Polypropylene
PVC – Polyvinylchloride
PSE – Polystyrene
PET – Polyester (polyethylene terephthalate: try saying that if you are not a chemist!)

Luckily, they are usually known by their initials.

The plastics' raw materials (called polymers) usually come in granule or powder form. They are then converted using heat and pressure on special processing machinery to produce bottles, tubs, films, crates, etc.

Thirty years ago plastic bottles used to look cloudy and we could easily distinguish them from glass bottles. But scientists have now learnt how to stretch plastics in a special way to make them clearer and tougher. PET bottles for fizzy drinks are made in this way. Films too can be stretched (in a different way) and, for example, another plastic, nylon, is used for boil-in-bag foods such as frozen fish (their sharp bones might puncture other films). Stretched PET film is used as oven roasting bags for cooking chickens at oven temperatures up to 200°C.

Paper and board

Paper and board are made from wood pulp (which comes from fibres found in trees) and waste paper. Board is manufactured in the same way as paper but it is thicker and heavier.

Worldwide, of the trees that are cut down each year, nearly three-quarters are removed to clear land for agriculture or used as fuel. The rest are used for commercial logging, producing timber for building and products like furniture and toys. The majority of paper is made from softwood trees which are grown and managed in forests specifically planted for this purpose.

Paper is mainly used for paper bags and labels and as one of the layers in lamination (layers of paper, foil or plastics bound together). Board is used in cartons and drums. Another product is corrugated board which is made from layers of paper and used where strong protection is needed, as in packing cases for electrical goods (television, radios, cookers, etc.) and for chemicals, books, pharmaceuticals and food packs. Because of the 'fluting' (the wavy layer in some cardboard boxes), it can absorb reasonable impact, making it especially useful for transport by road, air or sea. We recycle considerable quantities of paper and board in the UK. Most of it is used to make paper and board for packaging.

Paper and board packaging is useful because:

- the materials are light and easy to handle, store, fold and crease
- if combined with foil or plastic to

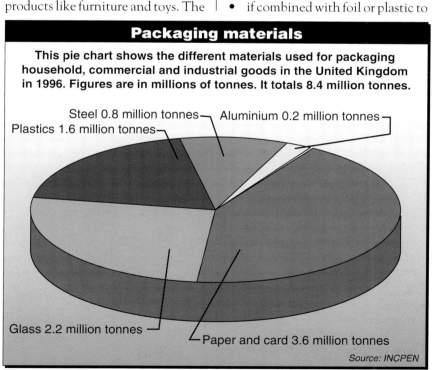

Packaging materials

This pie chart shows the different materials used for packaging household, commercial and industrial goods in the United Kingdom in 1996. Figures are in millions of tonnes. It totals 8.4 million tonnes.

Steel 0.8 million tonnes
Aluminium 0.2 million tonnes
Plastics 1.6 million tonnes
Glass 2.2 million tonnes
Paper and card 3.6 million tonnes

Source: INCPEN

form laminated packaging, special features are possible such as a seal that prevents evaporation and preserves the product
- colour printing to a very high quality is possible.

Metals

Steel and aluminium are used a great deal in packaging, to produce cans, aerosols, foil containers and metal closures. There are various ways to make cans. Some cans are made of three pieces of metal (steel) – most food cans are of this type. Other cans are made from two pieces of metal (either aluminium or steel) and are used mainly for pet foods and drinks. About half of these drinks cans are made from aluminium, the others from steel.

More than 15 thousand million food, pet food and drinks cans are bought every year, with most homes using about 14 cans every week.

Can you think of some of the advantages of canning food?

1. Canned food keeps well. As long as the cans are kept in a cool, dry cupboard, the food will last for many months or years.
2. It is very convenient because the food has already been cooked and can be eaten straight from the can or reheated without further preparation.
3. There is no need to add preservatives to canned food because the cooking and canning process preserves the contents until it is opened.
4. No food is wasted. (Well, do you leave any beans or peaches at the bottom of the tin?)
5. Drinks cans are a convenient size, and are easily opened, lightweight and easy to chill.

The food canning process

The stages in canning are:
1. The food is prepared for canning.
2. The cans are cleaned by powerful jet blowers and rinsed in purified water.
3. As the open cans move along a conveyor belt, the food is put into them and a liquid (brine for vegetables; syrup or fruit juice for fruit) is added.
4. They are then moved on to a can-closing machine and sealed. Each can is checked to make sure it has the right content level: any shortfilled cans are automatically rejected.
5. The cans are placed into a machine rather like a giant pressure cooker. The food is cooked and sterilised and the cans are cooled.
6. The conveyor moves on again. At this stage the cans are usually packed in 24s and the outer packaging is put on. They are placed by machine on cardboard trays and the whole pack is then shrink-wrapped in film and heat-sealed. Some cans are packed in cases made from corrugated board.
7. The final stage comes when the trays are loaded onto pallets and taken to a warehouse. Lorries collect them and take them to shops and supermarkets through-out the country.

Glass

Glass is one of the oldest of the packaging materials So old, that collectors go around antique shops, searching for old beer and other bottles. Today, glass-making is a huge business and glass is a very popular choice for some foods.

The advantages of glass are:
- you can see the contents clearly
- glass bottles and jars can be opened and resealed easily
- glass does not affect the taste of the food inside
- glass is impermeable, which means that liquids and gases cannot leak into or out of it
- some glass containers can be washed and reused
- the raw materials used to make glass (sand, limestone, soda ash) are cheap and in plentiful supply
- used bottles and jars can be saved in 'bottle banks' and recycled in a furnace to make more glass.

Can you think of any other advantages? What about the disadvantages? Can you think of any?

One of the problems with glass is its heaviness compared with other materials. Another is that glass can break.

- The above is an extract from the web site of the Industry Council for Packaging and the Environment (INCPEN) which can be found at www.incpen.org.uk

What to do at home

Your local authorities are making recycling your steel cans easier and easier! Not only do steel cans sometimes get recycled without you even knowing it, but some local authorities are bringing it around the corner or, for some, to your front doorstep!

So next time you open a can of baked beans, a can of lemonade, a can of pet food, or a can of beer STOP, and KNOW where you're recycling your steel cans!

Bring schemes

Save-a-Can

Save-a-Can is the nationwide can-collection scheme which, uniquely, accepts all types of food, drinks, pet food and aerosol cans. There are some 2000 Save-a-Can banks across the UK, serving some 26 million people. Managed by Corus in partnership with local authorities, these can banks will take any of the cans found in a typical cupboard at home. By locating the banks in central areas of towns and cities, as well as super-market car parks, special journeys can be avoided, thus saving further energy and resources.

The familiar blue and white Save-a-Can banks complement the magnetic extraction scheme. As Save-a-Can increases its operations, economies of scale enable the system to become more cost-effective and flexible. Increasingly, Save-a-Can is being adopted and run by local authorities to help them achieve their own recycling targets.

How to use Save-a-Can

Save-a-Can banks are easy to use. Just squash your cans (to enable more cans to be deposited in the bank and help make the scheme more efficient) and pop them into your local Save-a-Can bank. You don't even need to sort the steel cans from the aluminium ones because Save-a-Can recycles both metals.

What happens to the cans?

When a Save-a-Can bank is full, it is emptied and the cans are taken for sorting and recycling. All the collected aluminium and steel cans are taken to a regional depot until there are enough cans for them to be efficiently transported for recycling.

The cans are then transported to a processing plant where they are magnetically separated and then compacted into bales. The baled steel cans are then taken to a Corus steel making plant, to be made into new steel.

Independent can banks

In addition to the Save-a-Can scheme, there are a number of can bank schemes throughout the UK, which are run independently by local authorities or community collection projects.

Kerbside collection

Kerbside collection is another method of recovering recyclable materials which operates in many parts of the UK, which allows you to recycle from your doorstep.

In some areas of the country local authorities provide separate dustbins or boxes for different materials. This is known as kerbside collection, as the materials are collected from your doorstep. Kerbside collection of steel cans has increased by more than 60% over the past 3 years.

The kerbside schemes collect mixed materials, achieving high recovery rates for all materials. Once you have finished with your packaging – steel cans, paper, glass bottles, etc – rather than throwing it in the rubbish bin, all you have to do is keep it separate from your rubbish.

Different councils have different containers in which recyclable materials can be collected; some use coloured sacks, others coloured boxes. Once the recyclable items have been saved and put out for collection, they are taken to local sorting depots where each material is returned to the appropriate recycling plant.

• The above is information from the Steel Can Recycling Information Bureau (SCRIB) web site which can be found at www.scrib.org SCRIB is funded and run by Corus Steel Packaging Recycling.

© Steel Can Recycling Information Bureau (SCRIB)

Motivations to recycle

Those that do recycle are largely motivated by their belief in the environmental benefits of recycling – mentioned by just under half (46%). People feel good that they are 'doing their bit' for the environment, and conversely, feel guilty if they do not recycle. There is a particularly strong association between recycling paper and trees: people are able to visualise trees being chopped down, increasing the guilt factor and people's motivations to recycle paper. Paper is thought by four in ten (43%) to be the most important material to recycle because of this association. This suggests that developing associations between other materials and the environment could also help motivate people to recycle.

Recycling that benefits charities is an added benefit to recycling that motivated people to participate. Pressure from children is also a motivating factor, even if parents themselves do not believe in the merits of recycling.

• The above is an extract from the findings of a MORI poll on the issue of recycling.

© MORI

Glass recycling

The weekly trip to the local bottle bank is now a regular feature for millions of British households, but what lies behind the bottle bank system, how does it work, who benefits, and what does it achieve? Information from British Glass

The story so far . . .

Bottle banks appeared for the first time in the UK in 1977. There are now over 20,000 bottle bank sites in the UK – one for every 2,800 people. The average glass bottle contains over 25% recycled glass. Green glass bottles manufactured in this country contain at least 60%, and sometimes as much as 90%, recycled glass. In 1997 425,000 tonnes of glass was recycled in the UK.

Waste 2000: the challenge

In 1986 the government challenged the glass industry to double the number of bottle bank sites from 2,500 to 5,000 within 5 years – this was achieved a year early. In 1990 the challenge rose to 10,000 by 1995. The industry then set itself the goal of 20,000 bottle bank sites as soon as possible, and this has now been achieved.

The most recent challenge set by the government is for the packaging industry to recover 50% of packaging waste (glass bottles, paper cartons, aluminium cans etc.) by the year 2001. This complies with the targets set by the European Union in the Packaging and Packaging Waste Directive. Exact figures aside, the general message being put across by politicians in both London and Brussels is that recycling waste packaging is an environmentally responsible step that everyone can take part in.

Getting the message across

Children are often viewed as the ambassadors of environmental issues and to get the message on glass recycling across to them, an educational play called *Bottle Busters* tours primary schools in the UK. Over one and a half million primary school children have now seen *Bottle Busters* which recently celebrated its 10th birthday. A number of politi-cians have also seen the play – including Lady Thatcher.

The recycling cycle

What happens to the glass that we put into the bottle bank? Where does it go?

Firstly, all unwanted non-glass materials are rejected then the collected bottles and jars are crushed into cullet (the industry's term for used glass).

The clean cullet is then sent to the glass container manufacturer where it is mixed and fed into a furnace with additional raw materials. The high temperatures involved in the melting process destroy any secondary decoration technique on the recycled glass such as paint and ink left in the mix. As the molten glass is drawn from the furnace it is channelled through a 'feeder' mechanism into the bottle-making machines.

Once the bottles have been formed they undergo a series of automatic inspections and quality-control checks and are then sent to the filler. Once filled they are distributed to the retailer, and subsequently to the consumer with whom the cycle begins anew.

The quality of a recycled glass container is the same as the quality of the one which was first taken from the shelf at the beginning of the process. Recycled glass packaging is used in all market sectors from wine and beer to spirits and foods. Glass can be recycled indefinitely without any loss of quality.

Why recycle glass?

There are five main reasons to recycle glass:

Reason One

Glass recycling cuts waste disposal costs. Glass makes up about 8% by weight of our household refuse and any increase in the amount of glass recycled means savings on waste collection and waste disposal costs,

which are likely to increase due to the landfill tax. It also extends the life of our landfill sites therefore conserving the British countryside.

Reason Two
Glass recycling saves energy. The amount of energy needed to melt recycled glass is considerably less than that needed to melt virgin raw materials to make new glass.

Reason Three
Glass recycling conserves the environment. Using recycled glass in furnaces saves hundreds of thousands of tonnes of primary raw materials each year. This reduces the need for quarrying of raw materials, thereby conserving the countryside.

Reason Four
Glass recycling creates employment. A number of purpose-built recycling centres have been set up in the mainland UK to clean and process cullet. These centres provide employment and collection schemes and also create local jobs.

Reason Five
Glass recycling increases public awareness of the problem of waste and the benefits of recycling. Each individual can play an active part in conservation by simply supporting bottle banking. This is a first step towards becoming an environmentally aware consumer.

The glass code
The following hints and tips are designed to ensure that glass is recycled in the right way to make the job easier for both the consumer and the industry.

1. Always take refillable bottles, with or without a deposit, back to the supplier. Never put milk bottles in a glass recycling bottle bank – always return them to the milkman.
2. Before putting glass into bottle banks, empty and rinse the containers and remove any bottle caps or corks.
3. At the bottle bank, separate clear, brown and green glass and place into the appropriate bottle banks. Place blue bottles in the green bottle bank.

UK glass recycling figures

Total glass including flat recycled in 1998:	574,000 tonnes
Total glass packaging recycled in 1998:	476,000 tonnes
National production of glass in 1998:	1.83m tonnes
Percentage of glass packaging recycled:	22%
Percentage of glass recycled including flat:	27%
European average recycled:	Over 50%
Number of districts with bottle bank sites:	426
Total number of bottle bank sites at end of 1998:	22,821
Current number of public bottle bank sites:	17,291
Current number of commercial bottle bank sites:	4,530
Bottles and jars in a tonne:	Approx. 3,000
Bottles and jars in a kilo:	Approx. 3
Year of first bottle bank scheme:	1977
Glass as a percentage of the average household dustbin:	8-10%
Current ratio of bottle bank sites per head of population:	1:2,700

Source: 1999 British Glass Ltd.

4. Only deposit glass containers such as bottles and jars – food, pharmaceutical and household items packaged in glass are all recyclable as well as beer and wine bottles.
5. Never deposit window glass, light bulbs, Pyrex or Visionaware cooking dishes or glass crockery items in the bottle banks.
6. If a bottle is decorated, i.e. coated with printing inks, paints or a plastic sleeve, look at the top of the bottle or jar where the cap has been and see what colour the glass is to determine which bank to put it in.
7. Try to plan your trip to the bottle bank along with other essential errands such as shopping or school runs.
8. Don't leave cardboard boxes or plastic carrier bags used to bring the glass to the bottle bank unless there is a bin for these materials on site.
9. Never go to the bottle bank late at night as your visit may disturb local residents.
10. If you find your bottle bank is full, please try again another day.
11. Persuade a friend or relative to recycle glass too, and help the environment!

Fast facts/did you know?
- Jars and bottles are now made thinner and just as strong using less glass material, less raw material and making energy savings in the process.
- Glass is 100% recyclable.
- The colour of the glass is partly determined by the iron content of the different types of sand used as raw materials.
- The largest furnaces can produce more than 400 tonnes of glass a day which could equate to more than one million bottles/jars a day.
- It takes less energy to melt recycled glass than to melt virgin raw materials to make new glass.
- One bottle bank or igloo can hold up to 3,000 bottles before it needs to be emptied.
- On average, every family in the UK consumes around 500 glass bottles and jars every year – however we recycle less than 25% of these items.
- Every year around 2 million tonnes of glass is consumed in the UK but only 440,000 tonnes are recycled.
- Glass makes up around 8% by weight of our household refuse.

© 1999 British Glass Ltd.

Aluminium cans

Facts and info

The aluminium can is the most recycled drinks package in the UK.

Alcan has invested £28 million in the UK's only dedicated used aluminium drinks can recycling plant in Warrington, Cheshire – the plant is the largest in Europe. The plant produces 8-metre-long 26-tonne ingots which make 1.6 million aluminium cans. If you were to drink one can per day it would take nearly 4000 years to have used enough to form one ingot!

Where does aluminium come from?

Aluminium is the third most abundant element found in the earth's crust, after oxygen and silicon. Sir Humphrey Davy established the existence of aluminium in 1807. However, at this time it was so difficult to extract that aluminium was considered a semi-precious metal – so rare and expensive that Emperor Napoleon had a dinner service made from it!

It wasn't until 1886 that an economically viable process was developed to extract aluminium, independently achieved by both Charles Martin Hall and Paul L. T. Heroult.

A naturally occuring ore called bauxite is mined using an open-cast method with large mechanical diggers. The bauxite is then processed chemically to produce aluminium oxide. Smelting electrolysis is then employed to form molten aluminium, which is moulded to create large ingots of solid aluminium.

Here are some points worth considering . . .

- In 1998, over 60% of all drinks cans sold were made of aluminium.
- In 1998, recyclers were paid nearly £10 million for the aluminium cans they collected.
- In the UK in 1998 over 4 billion aluminium drinks cans were sold – if they were all collected for

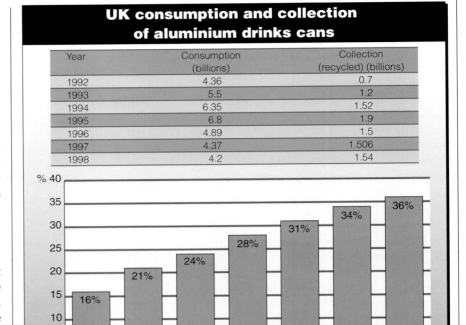

UK consumption and collection of aluminium drinks cans

Year	Consumption (billions)	Collection (recycled) (billions)
1992	4.36	0.7
1993	5.5	1.2
1994	6.35	1.52
1995	6.8	1.9
1996	4.89	1.5
1997	4.37	1.506
1998	4.2	1.54

Bar chart (%): 1992 16%, 1993 21%, 1994 24%, 1995 28%, 1996 31%, 1997 34%, 1998 36%

Source: Alupro

recycling over £38 million would have been paid to collectors.

- If all of the aluminium cans recycled in the UK in 1998 were laid end to end they would stretch from Land's End to John O'Groats 160 times, with some to spare!
- Aluminium packaging accounts for 2% by weight but 50% by value of materials collected for recycling. It has the highest value of any recyclable packaging material.
- There would be 12 million fewer full dustbins per annum in the UK if all aluminium drinks cans were recycled!
- Aluminium cans cool quicker than any other drinks package, allowing bars, hotels etc. to serve cold, fresh drinks sooner.
- The aluminium industry has invested over £60 million in the development of alucan recycling over the past eight years.
- In 1989 only 2% of aluminium cans consumed in the UK were recycled – in 1998 over 36% were recycled.

- Children and their parents are especially aware that money can be made from aluminium can 'empties' and are the most active recyclers.
- Industry demand for recycled alucans will always be strong and, whenever possible, industry operates 'closed loop' recycling, i.e. turning used aluminium cans into new can sheet.

About Alupro . . .

The Aluminium Packaging Recycling Organisation (Alupro) is funded by the major aluminium can and foil rollers, and the leading foil converters. Alupro's primary objective is to increase the recycling rate for aluminium drinks cans and foil. Since 1989 this has been done by promoting the fundraising and environmental benefits of aluminium can recycling. Since a national aluminium can recycling scheme was launched in 1989, alucan recycling rates have increased.

© Alupro

Recycling aluminium cans

Frequently asked questions. Information from Alupro

Why should I recycle alucans?
Recycling aluminium drinks cans saves up to 95% of energy used in primary production, natural resources are saved and the demand on landfill is reduced. Used aluminium drinks cans are valuable; collecting them for recycling is a great way to raise funds. If all the aluminium cans sold in the UK this year were to be recycled over £30million would be paid to the collectors.

How do I start to recycle my aluminium drinks cans?
Find out where your nearest alucan Cash for Cans Recycling Centre is located (telephone 0845 722 7722), sort your alu cans from steel and take them to your nearest Recycling Centre, where you will get paid cash.

How do I identify alucans from other cans?
One of three ways:
* look for the 'alu' symbol on the side of the can
* they do not stick to magnets
* they have shiny bases.

How do I find out where my nearest Recycling Centre is?
Call 0845 7 227722 (local rate) for a list of your nearest Centres (UK).

How much will I get paid for my aluminium cans?
Recycling Centres pay by weight. The price does fluctuate, however the average price paid is 40 pence per kilo. There are approximately 60 alucans in each kilo. Some Recycling Centres offer a collection service; if they collect from you they will usually pay slightly less.

Is there a minimum amount of alucans I can recycle at a Recycling Centre?
No – you can recycle as few or as many as you wish. However, it makes the administration process easier if you recycle at least one kilo (approx. 60 cans).

If there is not a Recycling Centre in my area, where can I recycle my cans?
You can put them into any can bank, normally situated in supermarket car parks.

How can I find out where my nearest can bank is?
Contact your Local Council – their telephone number will be listed in your local telephone directory.

What do I do with the steel cans?
These can be put into Savacan banks normally situated in supermarket car parks.

Do I need to crush my cans?
No – however, many people crush them to save space.

Where can I obtain can crushers?
These can be purchased from Stephens (Midlands) Ltd, Greets Green Industrial Estate, West Bromwich B70 9EW. Telephone 0121 522 2221 Fax 0121 557 6861.

Where can I obtain a collection container?
Try to reuse an old bin or box, or reuse carrier bags. Cardboard collection boxes can be purchased from Unex Design Ltd, Woodland Business Park, Torquay, Devon TQ2 7AT. Telephone 01803 612772. Facsimile 01803 613875

Can I recycle aluminium foil?
Yes – you can obtain further details by calling us on 0845 722 7722, or visit our aluminium foil website at www.alufoil.co.uk
  To find out more, call 0845 722 7722. Calls charged at UK local rate.

© Alupro

Aluminium cans and the environment

There are sound environmental benefits associated with recycling aluminium drinks cans. Here are just a few . . .

* Up to 95% of the energy needed to produce new aluminium ore is saved by recycling.
* By recycling alucans waste is reduced, thereby reducing pressure on landfill sites – the streets are kept a little tidier.
* Aluminium can be recycled time and time again without loss of quality.
* Aluminium drinks cans are lightweight, unbreakable, quick-chilling and energy saving in both use and through recycling.
* The 'closed loop' recycling process can happen in as little as six weeks!
* Over 50% of all aluminium drinks cans sold worldwide are recycled, making the alucan the world's most recycled package.
* If all the aluminium cans sold in the UK were recycled, there would be 12 million fewer full dustbins.
* With a recycling rate of 36% (1998), the aluminium drinks can is the UK's most recycled drinks package.
* To find out more, call 0845 722 7722. Calls charged at UK local rate.

© Alupro

Reuse

Information from Waste Watch

Recycling waste is something that we can do when an item has reached the end of its life. But this is the third level of the waste management hierarchy. Before we think about recycling, there is a second tier: it is often possible to look at ways of extending this life by reuse. If a product is reused, in the same state, the product has gone through no additional manufacturing. So reusing means there is no more need for energy consumption and no extra raw materials are required.

Why is there a need for reuse?
Research published by the Department of the Environment in 1997 estimated UK waste from households at 27 million tonnes a year. It has been estimated that for every tonne of household waste, another 5 tonnes are created at the manufacturing stage and 20 tonnes at the site of initial extraction. Offices in the UK generate a further 15 million tonnes of waste every year. This ever-increasing demand for raw materials is depleting the world's natural resources and supplies of non-renewable energy.

The vast majority of Britain's waste is disposed of in landfill sites which are becoming scarce, and which are responsible for releases of carbon dioxide and methane contributing to global warming. Landfill sites can produce leachate which, unless properly managed, can contaminate the water supply. Incinerators give off dioxins that are potentially hazardous to health.

How does reuse work?
Many of us reuse already without knowing it – under the heading of reuse are repair, refill and refurbish.

Getting a pair of shoes reheeled is a common practice, but many of the things we use could be repaired, and have their life extended instead of being thrown away. Places like the Body Shop offer a refill scheme for their bottles – only for the same product again. Giving a sofa a fresh lease of life by refurbishing it can be just as good as buying a brand new one.

Some reuse many of us do all the time without thinking twice about it, like buying a second-hand car, for example, or choosing metal cutlery and ceramic crockery over disposable plastic and paper.

Many of us reuse already without knowing it – under the heading of reuse are repair, refill and refurbish

---

Charity shops are a good example of reuse – and they don't just take unwanted clothes either. They gratefully receive all sorts of things such as bric-a-brac, books, records and some will take electrical goods too.

Don't forget to close the loop by buying what you can from charity shops. Many bargains can often be found there, and with fashion going in cycles, they can be a good source of authentic items for the latest revival. In addition to their main stores on the high street, Oxfam have opened a series of specialist designer shops.

Some successful reuse projects around the country
Many washing machines, cookers and fridges are thrown away when they have plenty of useful life in them. CREATE, based in Liverpool, refurbishes these used white goods to a high standard. These refurbished machines are sold on at modest prices.

Bristol's Recycling Consortium encourages many local groups in all sorts of different reuse schemes, including the SOFA Project – a registered charity and Consortium member aiming to alleviate poverty by repairing and reusing household goods.

Save Waste and Prosper, (SWAP) is a consultancy and project-management organisation that specialises in sustainable resource management, waste minimisation and recycling. One of its projects is Community Re>Paint. There are currently 14 local schemes around the country. Unwanted paint is redistributed free of charge for reuse

– IN YEAR'S TO COME YOU ARE GOING TO THANK US FOR NOT USING DISPOSABLE NAPPIES!

(SPEAKING OF NAPPIES...)

SIMON KNEEBONE

to those in 'social need'. It works through dedicated drop-off points – such as the local DIY store – skips at civic amenity sites, facilities at council or parish offices, kerbside collection and direct delivery to the scheme's base.

Disposable nappies make up about 4% of household waste – 8,000,000 are thrown away every day. There is now an alternative to just using the old terry nappies: a nappy washing service. There are many around the country so to find out about your local service, contact the National Association of Nappy Services who can give you details.

What other options are there?

Practical ways to reuse

- Invest in a reusable shopping bag to take to the shops instead of using plastic bags.
- Pass on unwanted clothes and furniture to friends or charities and second-hand shops.
- Avoid using cling film and aluminium foil. Use a box with a lid instead.
- If you have to use batteries, use rechargeable ones wherever you can.
- For brown and white goods check whether spare parts are available locally, and when items break, try to repair them rather than replacing them.
- Avoid disposable products, e.g. nappies, tissues, face wipes, razors, paper and plastic cups, plates and cutlery, kitchen towels, serviettes, computer cartridges, cameras.
- Take old magazines to your local doctors' or dentists' surgery.
- Use washable nappies, sanitary towels and handkerchiefs.
- Many charity shops – and Boots – will accept unwanted glasses.
- Use a refillable ink pen rather than a disposable biro.
- Use old jars for storage – or for when making homemade jam or chutney.
- Reuse envelopes – purchase reuse labels.
- Take a packed lunch in a sandwich box rather than wrapping it in foil.

Waste Watch's 1999 survey, *What People Think about Waste*, showed that 4 out of 5 people reuse at least one type of material. Most commonly reused are plastic bags – 54% of respondents – then glass bottles and jars – 50% – a further 20% reuse plastic containers. Clothes and rags are reused by 13% of people, paper/newspaper by 7% and cardboard or cardboard boxes by 5% of those asked.

- The above information is an extract from the Waste Watch web site which can be found at www.wastewatch.org.uk

Composting

Information from Waste Watch

Compost forms as a result of the natural breakdown of organic material derived from living animals and plants. The 'breaking down' is aerobic, i.e. an oxygen-using process performed by the bacteria, fungi, insects and animals, which inhabit soil. In a compost heap these organisms generate heat as they decompose organic matter and break it into fine particles. Composting is nature's own and oldest method of waste disposal and soil fertilisation.

Traditionally, gardeners have created their own compost using leaves, grass, shrub clippings and other useful organic materials found in the garden. Applying compost to soils provides an excellent conditioner and mulch, which fertilises and provides soil structure, retains moisture and can restrict weed growth. Man-made compost is an alternative to the peat compost extracted from important natural wildlife sites.

In recent years there has been interest in the creation of garden compost from organic household waste, as a result of the growing awareness of the environmental problems created by the traditional disposal methods. In the UK about 20 million tonnes of domestic refuse is produced each year, which contains about 30% organic content, such as vegetable peelings, tea bags and food scraps.

Currently, 85% of domestic waste ends up in landfill sites, 10% is incinerated and 5% is recycled. Incineration leaves a residue of 25%-30% of the original mass, which may contain toxic chemicals and heavy metals, and which still has to be landfilled. The organic materials within a landfill are the main source of methane (a greenhouse gas responsible for global warming) and liquid which may enter and contaminate water supplies. However the amount of methane released and liquid seepage can be controlled by appropriate landfill management.

The creation of compost from organic household waste helps the government achieve its target of recycling 25% of all domestic waste. Individual households can help reach this target either by making their own compost or by participating in a centralised community scheme. The success of both home composting and centralised schemes is dependent upon the separation of organic (putrescible) waste from other waste.

Making your own compost

This can be done either by making a traditional compost heap, or by using a worm bin. There are numerous containers now on the market for making a compost heap, although perfectly satisfactory ones can be constructed from scrap timber, old tyres, bricks or wire mesh. Advice on making a compost heap is widely available through gardening books and magazines.

A worm bin is a container housing a colony of special types of worms, known as brandlings, tiger worms or redworms. Worm bins can be kept indoors (with careful management) or out, and are ideal for households with no gardens, as they produce only a small quantity of compost and a liquid, which forms a concentrated plant food. There are a variety of worm bins available for sale, complete with 'worm starter kits'. However it is possible to make your own, and suitable worms can be obtained from fishing shops. A useful leaflet is available from The Henry Doubleday Research Association.

Leaf mould can be made by placing leaves in a large black bag or in an open-topped wire cage. After one year they will form a mulch, and after two years a fine textured potting compost will be produced.

Centralised community composting schemes

Centralised composting schemes involve the collection and centralised processing of various organic wastes including: kitchen and garden waste separated by the householder; 'special garden waste' from private and public landscaping and park creation schemes; farm wastes; sewage sludge; and industrial food processing wastes. Many local authorities have carried out experiments to make a range of compost and mulch products from either one or a combination of these sources.

For example, collections of prunings and thinnings from land-scaping projects can be converted into wood chippings, which decompose to form mulches and composts. In the majority of situations, weeds, seeds and potentially harmful organisms do not have to be separated out as they will be killed by the heat produced during the 'breaking down' process.

Some schemes also involve the mixing of organic and non-organic material. The quality of the finished product is graded according to its organic purity for marketing purposes. Elimination of glass is the main prerequisite for the production

of compost for sale. Glass is extremely difficult to screen out and a small amount renders it difficult to sell directly to the public and impossible to sell through major distribution chains. Other contaminants are generally less common in the waste stream and are more easily screened.

The highest quality compost, which is contaminant free, is ideal for horticulture. Compost which is slightly contaminated with glass and plastics may be suitable for landscaping, tree planting, use in municipal parks and gardens or agricultural fertilisation (provided the land would not be used for grazing). The grossly contaminated compost derived from a combination of municipal solid wastes and sewage sludges can be utilised for land reclamation and restoration of landfill sites.

Large-scale, centralised schemes involve management, outlay and maintenance costs and are often dependent upon householders to sort their own domestic rubbish. However, the sale of compost and mulch products may offset production costs and the costs of alternative waste disposal methods. Householders who dispose of their own organic waste by creating their own compost do not impose any costs upon the local community.

Examples of community composting

East and North Hertfordshire

Since June 1993, 2,200 households in East and North Hertfordshire have had a second wheeled bin for organic waste collection, which is emptied fortnightly. The material is taken to a sealed composting site near Hertford, consisting of a disused agricultural Dutch Barn with hardstanding and a tank for the collection of run off. The material is shredded and placed into large compost heaps known as windrows, which are turned regularly to maintain a supply of oxygen to the micro-organisms.

After about twelve weeks the process is complete and biological activity in the windrow is reduced. The material is then screened into the appropriate particle sizes and

stored to mature before use as a mulch or soil conditioner on the Councils' parks and gardens contracts. The scheme has reached the target of recycling 25% of household waste, saving landfill space and avoiding the creation of methane.

Chelson Meadow landfill in Plymouth

For each 100 tonnes of municipal solid waste and sludge that enters the windrows at Chelson Meadow landfill in Plymouth, 49 tonnes of compost are produced. After about 35 days the materials are scooped up, passed through a screen to remove pieces larger than 8mm across, e.g. cans and plastic bottles, and left to mature in a new heap. Smaller contaminants, e.g. small pieces of glass and plastic, are still present, but the compost should be acceptable to the local farmers and developers.

Other schemes

WyeCycle – At Wye in Kent, a community scheme organises the collection of organic material from the villagers for the creation of compost for local use.

The London Borough of Sutton offers residents, in selected areas, the opportunity to buy compost makers (the worm bin, green cone, rotol converter) at special discount prices to encourage home composting.

Leeds City Council provides two split bins for the separate collection of dry recyclables and organic materials by its pilot kerbside collection scheme.

Gloucester City Council, in association with Garden Waste Recycling at Stroud, collects garden waste from public amenity sites which is composted and sold.

Seven North London Boroughs participate in a scheme to collect organic waste from parks, civic amenity sites, commercial and industrial premises and send it to a composting plant in Edmonton. The compost is packaged for sale under the brand name Dickenson's.

• The above information is an extract from the Waste Watch web site which can be found at www.wastewatch.org.uk
© Waste Watch

Energy from waste

A super renewable

Energy in our lives

Energy plays a vital role in every aspect of our lives.

There isn't a single moment in the day when we are not responsible for consuming energy. At work or at home, our lifestyles are sustained by energy in one form or another. Life without electric power would, for most of us, be simply unimaginable.

Energy is invisible, but its generation and efficient use are of fundamental importance to the modern world. Energy production through the burning of fossil fuels is a major source of emissions of carbon dioxide (CO_2). This is one of the 'greenhouse gases' now thought, with increasing certainty, to be the principal cause of global warming.

International agreement on the need for greenhouse gas reduction was reached at the 1997 Kyoto Conference, and UK Government policy is to reduce carbon emissions by 20% by 2010.

This ambitious target can only be achieved by reducing energy consumption, using energy more efficiently and generating a greater proportion from renewable sources which do not involve fossil fuel burning. The Government is aiming to generate 10% of energy from renewable sources by 2010.

Soon, all electricity consumers will be free to choose from among a range of suppliers, rather than just relying on their regional electricity company. Some will offer energy from renewable sources.

Renewable energy

Renewable energy can be generated in a number of ways. Chief among these are:

- Wind energy, generating electricity from wind turbines
- Combustion of residual waste (e.g. domestic waste after recycling) as a fuel
- Hydro-electric generation, or energy derived from water/wave power
- Using solar energy directly for heating
- Energy crops grown specially for use as a fuel
- Combustion of methane generated by landfilling untreated waste
- Photo-voltaic (PV) generation in which the action of light falling on a cell causes a current to flow.

Energy is invisible, but its generation and efficient use are of fundamental importance to the modern world

---

Waste combustion or energy from waste (EfW) is likely to play an essential role in meeting the Government's target. EfW has the following advantages:

- It is one of the cheapest sources of renewable energy
- It is carbon dioxide (CO_2) neutral, since the energy released by its combustion is derived almost wholly from renewable sources such as paper and green waste
- It helps to reduce the use of fossil fuels by displacing generation from their combustion. The small amount of plastics in household waste does not give rise to a net increase in CO_2 emissions
- It avoids the emission of methane, a greenhouse gas many times more powerful than CO_2 which results from landfilling untreated waste
- Power generation from waste is continuous and reliable.

Environmental issues

Waste continues to grow and we are running out of space in the countryside to use for landfilling.

However much we try to reduce waste and increase recycling, there will always be a substantial volume of waste for which the best option is energy recovery.

Waste-fired community heating schemes are already in operation in

---

Energy from waste

The average dustbin over one year contains enough energy for the following:

One year   =   500 baths or 3,500 showers   OR   5,000 television hours

Source: Energy from Waste Foundation

Nottingham and Sheffield, serving a growing number of houses and public buildings and bringing the greater efficiency of combined heat and power (CHP).

EfW technology produces useful energy more cleanly than conventional power stations – and is very different from the waste incinerators of the past.

Waste-fired power stations are tightly regulated to European standards – overseen by the Environment Agency – to make sure that they are safe. Advanced exhaust gas cleaning equipment, including dust filters, ensures that emissions are kept well inside the limits set. Local community representatives can inspect emission records at any time.

EfW plants are truly a 'win-win' solution, generating renewable energy and providing more sustainable waste management.

Energy from waste – the future

EfW is widely employed in Europe. An EU White Paper was published in 1997 calling for the development of renewable energy in Europe and proposing the doubling of generation from renewable sources including EfW to 12% by 2010.

Some 50 million tonnes of waste are combusted in Europe to produce energy.

Sweden recovers energy from 50% of its domestic waste and countries with strong environmental records such as Denmark and Switzerland actively use energy recovery.

In the UK, EfW is now growing from a low base. Already, nearly 200 megawatts is being generated from about two million tonnes of waste a year – enough power for a quarter of a million homes.

The potential of energy from waste is at least 750 megawatts of renewable energy.

What can you do?

Consider changing your electricity supplier to one that offers energy from renewable sources – including energy from waste.

Ask your local authority how much waste actually gets recycled, not just collected, and what plans it has for recovering energy from the remainder.

For further information about EfW, contact:

Energy from Waste Foundation (EFW), 26 Spring Street, London W2 1JA. Tel: 020 7402 7110. Fax: 020 7402 7115. E-mail: info@efw.bdx.co.uk

© Energy from Waste Foundation (EFW)

Plastics waste management

Information from the British Plastics Federation

Introducing plastics

From windsurf boards to window frames, and shopping bags to surgical stitches, plastics are playing their part in today's world. Plastics can be made from oil, natural gas, coal and salt. There are about 50 different types with their own characteristics and, depending on how the raw materials are processed, the products from which they are made can become as light and flexible as cling film or as tough as a hang glider. Qualities that have made plastics so popular are durability, light weight and resistance to moisture, chemicals and decay.

The potential of recycled plastics : a second life

Plastics recycling takes place on a significant scale in the UK and there is considerable research conducted to discover the most efficient ways to recycle. Raw materials have a high value and are a precious resource, so to conserve both money and the

environment the industry makes every effort to recover as much as possible.

Exact figures are hard to obtain but a survey conducted in 1981 showed that less than 1% of plastics processed is thrown away at the manufacturing stage. Further downstream many products that have completed a full service life are fed back into the system to embark upon a second life-cycle. The following are just some examples:

Polyethylene film

It is estimated that around 50,000 tonnes of polyethylene film, about 10% of total UK production, are recovered every year to provide useful and serviceable goods such as certain types of builders' sheeting and black refuse bags, the majority of which are made from recycled material.

Polypropylene

At least 25,000 tonnes of polypropylene are recycled annually, equivalent to about 7% of total UK

production. More than 70% of this material has had a full service life with major sources being bottle crates and car battery boxes. The recycled material is used in high-quality applications such as injection mouldings and extruded drainage pipes.

Polystyrene

Recycling of polystyrene clothes hangers collected from department stores is an excellent example of a successful commercial venture , as is a similar system based on the recovery of used cassette cases taken from photographic laboratories. Typical applications include injection moulded products, including recycled versions of the original article or quite different products such as flower pots.

Recycling plastics which have been through the domestic waste stream will prove more difficult and the economics are known to be less favourable. A hopeful indication for the future, however, is the successful recycling of mixed plastics which have been obtained from distributive trade wastes. Products currently fabricated from such materials include livestock penning and industrial flooring. Another possible route for domestic waste is the development of collection schemes which involve the consumer. Whatever the point of separation the issue is whether the recycling of domestic waste can be made economically viable.

Source of energy

Material recovery is by no means the only way to recycle plastics. Another option is to recover their thermal content, providing an alternative source of energy. An average typical value for polymers found commonly in household waste is 38 mega joules per kilogram (MJ/kg), which compares favourably to the equivalent value of 31 MJ/kg for coal. This represents a valuable resource raising the overall calorific value of domestic waste which can then be recovered through controlled combustion and reused in the form of heat and steam to power electricity generators. Successful ventures in this field include plants, such as a major incinerator in Edmonton, North London, which produces steam to power an electricity turbine. The electricity is then sold to the Eastern Electricity Board. Waste containing plastics can also be reprocessed to yield fuel pellets, which have the added advantage of being storeable.

It is sometimes claimed that incineration of municipal waste poses an environmental problem in the shape of atmospheric pollutants. Although the potential is there, modern incineration techniques ensure that actual emission levels are kept within internationally accepted safety limits. In fact, several countries, such as Sweden, Germany and the Netherlands, have recently affirmed their confidence in incineration by announcing plans to expand existing capacity.

Land reclamation

The majority of municipal waste is still used as landfill, due to the very high cost of facilities for the sorting, separation and recycling of waste.

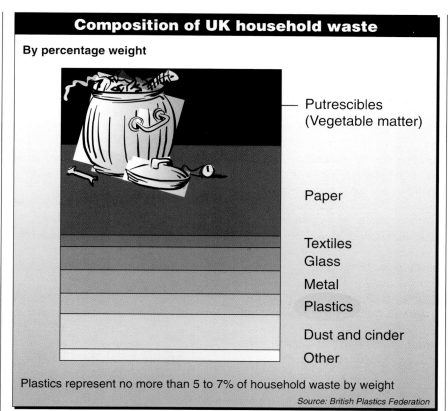

Composition of UK household waste

By percentage weight

- Putrescibles (Vegetable matter)
- Paper
- Textiles
- Glass
- Metal
- Plastics
- Dust and cinder
- Other

Plastics represent no more than 5 to 7% of household waste by weight

Source: British Plastics Federation

As plastics are stable, both physically and chemically, they in turn provide stability to the tips. This provides a safe and solid foundation upon which to build; thereby releasing land for development.

Conserving the environment

The plastics industry is concerned that it should take appropriate care of resources and the environment. The advantages of plastics over other raw materials are apparent from the beginning of their life-cycle. Research shows that it often takes less energy to make products in plastics, and although most plastics depend on oil, coal or gas they are responsible for only a small fraction of the national consumption of these fuels. In addition, as plastics are lighter and easier to store and transport, energy savings are made.

Plastics recycling takes place on a significant scale in the UK and there is considerable research conducted to discover the most efficient ways to recycle

---

As well as developments in the recycling of plastics, there have been interesting advances in the production of degradable plastics for products which need only a limited life.

The future

Plastics recycling is in the growth phase as the whole industry is still relatively young. A further development in recycling, which is being researched, is the recovery of the individual chemical components of plastics for reuse as chemicals, or for the manufacture of new plastics.

The British Plastics Federation is committed to encouraging industry to exploit the potential of plastics for recycling. It recognises that many of the measures that could be taken to increase recycling ventures are inhibited by both cost and practicalities. The BPF therefore sponsors research and seminars on recycling issues, to ensure innovation and development within the plastics industry.

• The above is information from the British Plastics Federation (BPF) web site which can be found at www.brf.co.uk
© British Plastics Federation (BPF)

Waste minimisation

Information from the World Resource Foundation

Waste minimisation is at the top of almost every version of a waste management hierarchy around the world, and is considered by many to be the most important management technique to be applied to solid wastes.

Despite that apparent importance, and with the exception of a few schemes conducted within particular companies and industries, most attention to date has been focused on finding ways of dealing with wastes once they have been created, rather than avoiding them.

That may be because, unlike post-creation management techniques such as reuse, recycling, composting or energy-from-waste initiatives, minimising the quantity of wastes actually produced during a particular process requires very specific knowledge of that process.

General recommendations, while helpful in theory, often contribute little in any individual case, over and above giving pointers as to possible waste reduction routes. In order to successfully reduce waste volumes, it is first necessary to establish the composition of that waste, and the reasons which prompted its creation.

In a domestic situation, those reasons may include or be dictated by lifestyle, for example if both parents are working full time, necessitating the purchase of more convenience foods, or if there is a young baby in the family using disposable nappies.

In a commercial situation, some waste may be the result of delivery policies set by a central supply system, or stem from choices made years before on types of machinery, requiring considerable investment in new equipment to change.

Since household waste is a very small percentage (typically in Europe perhaps only 6-10%) of total wastes created, it is apparent that individuals can have only a small impact on overall waste volumes, and that the biggest contribution to reducing wastes must come from manufacturing industry, from agriculture and from the construction and demolition sectors.

Having said that, there are important contributions which individuals can make, such as simply buying less, as well as choosing more durable products, and repairing or refurbishing old, worn or broken goods.

Saying what you mean

Much of the terminology used in connection with waste management is used by different people to mean entirely different things.

People say they have 'recycled' their glass and paper when they deposit it into banks, when actually they have only collected it. Recycling is a complex and lengthy process.

'Recycling' is also used to describe schemes which recover

...I'VE BEEN THINKING ABOUT MY LIFE STYLE -WASTE-STYLE ACTUALLY...

empty bottles for refilling, or which repair old furniture, when strictly those are examples of reuse.

Another example of terminology confusion is the phrase *waste minimisation*. While some consider the diversion of waste materials into recycling to be waste minimisation, since that reduces the amount of waste going for final disposal, the original intent of the term was *to reduce to a minimum the amount of waste being generated*.

Reusing or recycling that which is unavoidable is the next stage in the chain.

Conclusion

There are few instant solutions to reducing waste, but taking a wider view of what constitutes waste, and examining our actions as consumers, will help make best use of our resources.

Do we really need that electric toothbrush?

Have we asked to have our name removed from junk mailing lists?

Do we use public transport and car-share whenever possible?

By being aware of the impacts of purchasing decisions, both industry and individuals can make a difference to total resource consumption.

• The World Resource Foundation provides information on international sustainable management of municipal solid waste. WRF is totally independent of commercial vested interests and is a registered charity.

The Foundation publishes *Warmer Bulletin*, and is advised by a council of eminent specialists, all of whom give their services free of charge. The above information is an extract from the *Waste Minimisation Information Sheet*. There are other titles in the series produced by the World Resource Foundation. See page 41 for address details.

© *World Resource Foundation (WRF)*

ADDITIONAL RESOURCES

You might like to contact the following organisations for further information. Due to the increasing cost of postage, many organisations cannot respond to enquiries unless they receive a stamped, addressed envelope.

Aluminium Packaging Recycling Organisation (Alupro)
5 Gatsby Court
176 Holliday Street
Birmingham, B1 1TJ
Tel: 0121 633 4656
Fax: 0121 633 4698
E-mail: recycling@alucan.org.uk
Web site: www.alucan.org.uk
The Aluminium Packaging Recycling Organisation (Alupro) is the 'one-stop' shop in the UK for all matters relating to aluminium packaging including recycling schemes and reprocessing.

British Glass
Northumberland Road
Sheffield, S10 2UA
Tel: 0114 268 6201
Fax: 0114 268 1073
E-mail: recycling@britglass.co.uk
Web site: www.britglass.co.uk
British Glass maintains a directory of bottle bank sites and provides informations and advice on glass recycling.

British Plastics Federation
6 Bath Place
Rivington Street
London, EC2A 3JE
Tel: 020 7457 5000
Fax: 020 7457 5045
E-mail: haustin@bpf.co.uk
Web site: www.bpf.co.uk
The British Plastics Federation is fully committed to the use of recycling as part of an effective waste management strategy.

Energy from Waste Foundation
26 Spring Street
London, W2 1JA
Tel: 020 7402 7110
Fax: 020 7402 7115
E-mail: info@efw.bdx.co.uk
Web site: www.efw.org.uk
One of the Energy from Waste Foundation's principal aims is to increase awareness of the benefits of energy recovery from unavoidable waste, particularly that produced by households.

Going for Green
Elizabeth House
The Pier
Wigan, WN3 4EX
Tel: 01942 612621
Fax: 01942 824778
E-mail: gfg@dircon.co.uk
Web site: www.gfg.iclnet.co.org.uk
Going for Green encourages the public to adopt environmentally friendly lifestyles.

Industry Council for Packaging and the Environment (INCPEN)
Tenterden House
3 Tenterden Street
London, W1R 9AH
Tel: 020 7409 0949
Fax: 020 7409 0161
E-mail: info@incpen.org
Web site: www.incpen.org
INCPEN works for a better understanding of the role of packaging and a minimisation of the environmental impact of packaging.

National Recycling Forum
Europa House
Ground Floor
13-17 Ironmonger Row
London, EC1V 3QG
Tel: 020 7253 6266
Fax: 020 7253 5962
Web site: www.nrf.org.uk
The National Recycling Forum is an independent forum managed by Waste Watch.

Pulp and Paper Information Centre (PPIC)
1 Rivenhall Road, Westlea
Swindon, SN5 7BD
Tel: 01793 889600
Fax: 01793 886182
E-mail: ppic@paper.org.uk
Web site: www.ppic.org.uk
PPIC is committed to encouraging the responsible production, use and disposal of paper and board products. PPIC aims to unite the wider industry, enabling it to speak with one voice in open and honest communications.

Tidy Britain Group
Elizabeth House, The Pier
Wigan, WN3 4EX
Tel: 01942 824620
Fax: 01942 824778
E-mail: enquiries@tidybritain.org.uk
Web site: www.tidybritain.org.uk
Tidy Britain Group is a national charity committed to creating and maintaining high quality environments locally and nationally.

Waste Watch
Europa House, Ground Floor
13-17 Ironmonger Row
London, EC1V 3QG
Tel: 020 7253 6266
Fax: 020 7253 5962
E-mail: info@wastewatch.org.uk
Web site: www.wastewatch.org.uk
Waste Watch's inspiration and values derive from a desire to protect the environment by ensuring the sustainable use and disposal of scarce resources, primarily by advocating waste reduction, reuse and recycling of materials.

World Wide Fund For Nature (WWF-UK)
Panda House, Weyside Park
Catteshall Lane
Godalming, GU7 1XR
Tel: 01483 426444
Fax: 01483 426409
Web site: www.wwf-uk.org
WWF works with government, industry, media and the public to protect the decline in animal and plant species and reduce pollution.

Young People's Trust for the Environment and Nature Conservation (YPTENC)
8 Leapale Road
Guildford, GU1 4JX
Tel: 01483 539600
Fax: 01483 301992
E-mail: info@yptenc.org.uk
Web site: www.yptenc.org.uk
Works to educate young people in matters relating to the conservation of the world's wild places and natural resources.

INDEX

* * * * *

The Internet has been likened to shopping in a supermarket without aisles. The press of a button on a Web browser can bring up thousands of sites but working your way through them to find what you want can involve long and frustrating on-line searches.

And unfortunately many sites contain inaccurate, misleading or heavily biased information. Our researchers have therefore undertaken an extensive analysis to bring you a selection of quality Web site addresses.

Friends of the Earth
www.foe.co.uk
Friends of the Earth is the largest international network of environmental groups in the world, represented in 61 countries. They have a variety of waste and recycling-related information on their site.

Waste Watch
www.wastewatch.org.uk
Waste Watch is the national organisation that educates, informs and raises awareness on waste reduction, reuse and recycling. Click on the Information button for a wide range of articles on waste and recycling.

Aluminium Packaging Recycling Organisation
www.alucan.org.uk
Recycling aluminium drinks cans saves up to 95% of energy used in primary production, natural resources are saved and the demand on landfill is reduced. A useful site for information.

Tidy Britain Group
www.tidybritain.org.uk
Click on the Information button for everything you ever wanted to know about litter but didn't know who to ask!

British Glass
www.britglass.co.uk
Click on Glass Recycling for a range of useful information.

ACKNOWLEDGEMENTS

The publisher is grateful for permission to reproduce the following material.

While every care has been taken to trace and acknowledge copyright, the publisher tenders its apology for any accidental infringement or where copyright has proved untraceable. The publisher would be pleased to come to a suitable arrangement in any such case with the rightful owner.

Chapter One: The Problems of Waste

Rubbish, © Young People's Trust for the Environment, *Household rubbish problem is piling up*, © Telegraph Group Limited, London 1999, *What is waste?*, © Industry Council for Packaging and the Environment (INCPEN), *What do we mean by waste?*, © HTI, *What is waste?*, © Crown copyright is reproduced with the permission of the Controller of Her Majesty's Stationery Office, *Facts on waste*, © Crown copyright is reproduced with the permission of the Controller of Her Majesty's Stationery Office, *Britain to be 'swamped' by rubbish*, © The Independent, July 1999, *The management of wastes*, © Environment Agency, *Estimated annual waste in the UK by sector*, Crown copyright is reproduced with the permission of the Controller of Her Majesty's Stationery Office, *The present day*, © Waste Watch, *Why does society have a problem with waste?*, © HTI, *Stresses and strains*, © Environment Agency, *Britain's load of rubbish getting bigger and bigger*, © The Guardian, July 1999, *Cutting the waste we generate*, © Crown copyright is reproduced with the permission of the Controller of Her Majesty's Stationery Office.

Chapter Two: Reducing Waste

Doing your bit for reducing waste, © Going for Green/Tidy Britain Group, *Rubbish*, © Young People's Trust for the Environment, *War on waste*, © The World Wide Fund for Nature, *Recycling*, © The World Wide Fund for Nature, *What is recycling?*, © Going for Green/Waste Watch, *What is recycled?*, © Going for Green/Waste Watch, *Rubbish rebate aims to reward recyclers*, © The Guardian, February 1999, *Worldwide recycling figures*, © The Guardian, February 1999, *Recycling – the facts*, © Pulp and Paper Information Centre, *Britain fails to hit recycling target*, © Telegraph Group Limited, London 1999, *What can we recycle?*, © Waste Watch, *Buy recycled – an introduction*, © National Recycling Forum, *Make the pledge to buy recycled!*, © Going for Green/Tidy Britain Group, *Understanding terminology*, © National Recycling Forum, *Is your rubbish rubbish?*, Crown copyright is reproduced with the permission of the Controller of Her Majesty's Stationery Office, *Materials for packaging*, © Industry Council for Packaging and the Environment (INCPEN), *Packaging materials*, © Industry Council for Packaging and the Environment (INCPEN), *What to do at home*, © Steel Can Recycling Information Bureau (SCRIB), *Motivations to recycle*, © MORI, *Glass recycling*, © 1999 British Glass Ltd, *UK glass recycling figures*, © 1999 British Glass Ltd, *Aluminium cans*, © Alupro, *UK consumption and collection of aluminium drinks cans*, © Alupro, *Recycling aluminium cans*, © Alupro, *Aluminium cans and the environment*, © Alupro, *Reuse*, © Waste Watch, *Composting*, © Waste Watch, *Energy from waste*, © Energy from Waste Foundation (EFW), *Energy from waste*, © Energy from Waste Foundation (EFW), *Plastics waste management*, © British Plastics Federation, *Composition of UK household waste*, © British Plastics Federation, *Waste minimisation*, © World Resource Foundation.

Photographs and illustrations:

Pages 1, 5, 12, 14, 19, 23, 30: Pumpkin House, pages 3, 10, 16, 21, 24, 28, 34, 40: Simon Kneebone.

Craig Donnellan
Cambridge
May, 2000